THIS BOOK

BELONGS TO

Tara Austin

The Book of Life

Nick Austin

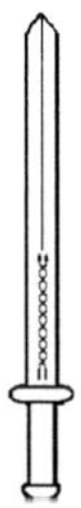

OGMIUM PRESS

First published on 5th May 2003
By Ogmium Press
Landscape Studios, Crowhurst, East Sussex TN33 9BX
Printed and bound in Great Britain
By Antony Rowe Limited, Eastbourne BN23 6QT

Pen and ink graphics by Tara Austin
Affirmation page design taken from the
William Blake woodcut "The Divine Image"
From "Songs of Innocence and Experience"
1789 - 1794

A CIP catalogue record of this book
Is available from the British Library

ISBN 0 - 9544801 - 0 - 4

A paperback version of this book is available
www.ogmium.com

THE AUTHOR

Nick Austin is the Chairman of the Landscape Channel - a television channel which shows the beauty of nature to the accompaniment of the world's greatest classical and instrumental music without advertising.

In 1986 he experienced a life-changing event which started him on a path of discovery, which would eventually lead to the writing of the Book of Life.

Over the seventeen years he was guided to the inevitable conclusion that the source of his visions had access to knowledge that could not be known to any mortal. These in turn led to the creation of the Book of Life. A work that the writer claims no authorship or credit, other than the act of service, since in his own words he "*received these words in spirit, knowing that those things that are written here are nothing more than any man should be able to understand*"

A Template for life

The Book of Life

This book is a philosophy of life. In the wider sense this is a book of the way of life, a book that reveals the fundamental truth of who you are. A book that shows those who are ready the way forward for their lives in the grander scheme of that great humanity that surrounds us. This book is therefore an understanding of life, which explains why we are here and how we should conduct ourselves in our daily experience. Like all philosophies it is a basis for human understanding of who we are – it is the definitive attempt to write down how we, as society, should live now that we have started to grow up inside. It is a template of life in the new millennium – the Ten Commandments for the modern man or woman.

In order to understand this philosophy you must first be a seeker of truth. Truth has been denied us by our own ignorance over many centuries. The time for the awakening of human consciousness is arriving. This process started many centuries ago and can be witnessed throughout human history. This raising of consciousness is witnessed by the fact that human brains and metabolism have changed little in the last ten thousand years. None the less we see man moving inexorably from a state of feudal ignorance to one of moral understanding and eventually a state of balance with himself and nature. A state where weapons were once the only form of enforcement, to one where the pen or mind can now be mightier than the sword. A state where true happiness can exist for everyone.

Whilst it may be argued that there are many places on this planet where the sword still reigns supreme over the pen, it cannot be denied that human consciousness is rising. This book comes as a response to that initiative. Science alone cannot answer the most fundamental questions we ask ourselves or understand how the mind works. Science, whilst flattering itself into believing there is a scientific answer to all questions, may be good at observing external events, however it is completely inadequate when confronted with how we work inside our existence. Science cannot explain where *"I"* go during sleep and has therefore created the myth called "*consciousness*", which has no basis in science at all.

Let us first therefore look at the concepts of who we are and what we are and then we may start to understand why we are here. These are probably the most important questions that you may ever ask yourself. They are the sorts of questions you ask yourself when your life is in crisis, you may also ask these same questions when you are young and, more frequently, just before you die. These are important questions that you should know the answers to in your life here and now. The answers to these questions do not need to be answered in the language of religion, designed to ensnare you into a church, or religious dogma. They do not need you to believe in some magical life after death, in heaven or anything outside of your own experience. All you need to do is to take the time to follow those instincts that are natural to you and a time will come when you will understand. Taking the time to read this book is the first indication that your time of understanding is approaching.

Over the centuries we, as human beings, have been indoctrinated by religious organisations. Humanity has been led by one religion or another, depending upon where you may live, or at what time in history. One religion may promise life after death in the form of everlasting heaven, another may promise bliss if you die for their particular cause. Many others offer everlasting salvation if you hand over your soul during your short stay on this earth into the care of their organisation – usually to the accompaniment of payment in some form or other.

Man shows throughout history that he has an inner need to find and understand the concept of God. This deep instinctual desire is like a shadow on his heart when the sun sets. A deeply held belief in something that he cannot see or put his finger on but knows is there. Unable to see in the dark he imagines what he believes to be true. He has created form and structure of religious institutions, faith and dogma, so strong that he is prepared to fight and die for this vision, which he cannot see, and never has seen. He has identified a human timeless force he calls his *spirit* or *soul,* which is bound into the religious doctrines. In this darkness he waits for the dawn, when the rays of enlightenment will show him the truth, whilst those same institutions flourish and multiply across the globe, fearful of the different contradictions held by different faiths.

All religions cannot be true by their contradictory nature and in truth many must therefore be completely wrong. Any religion that claims itself to be the only correct religion cannot in itself be correct - because God is not selective in His creations – He made all of us in the philosophical sense, including all forms of life, matter and religions. If God exists then why does he not show himself and why does a Buddhist see Buddha when in a state of Divine revelation, yet only Christ will reveal himself to a Christian in a similar state?

The answer of course is that we all have, and have had since the beginning of time, an inner need to be reunited with our maker and therefore express our inner beliefs as external apparitions when such matters arise. God does not exist as an external physical entity, but exists inside our minds and all things that exist. This is the reason there is no man who has ever lived upon this planet who has claimed to see God. Not even Christ – who constantly referred to his Father, as an analogy of the Divine Spirit. When the scriptures are re-read in this context a much wider understanding of Christ's teachings are understood.

God is not a Christian God, a Muslim Allah, a Jewish Jehovah or a Hindu god. God is all of these things and is in essence one Divine Spirit. A spiritual force that exists in the space in between and inside every atom known and unknown in our existence. A Divine Spirit capable of expressing itself through you and in you, both inside you and outside of you, through the world that you live in. You are the Divine Spirit's instrument of existence, along with every other living and inanimate object in the Universe. The enlightened spirit knows this in their heart, since it is the application of not just common sense, but inner knowledge – confirming your need to better understand who you are. To blindly accept one religion as an act of "*faith*" is to deny yourself the true knowledge of who you are, by excluding other religious belief systems. The very contradiction of this act of denial means that the "*faith*" you have been indoctrinated with must by its very nature be false – because God excludes none from his creation. Only a man can have the arrogance to claim the authority of God. Any religious belief system based upon a man, or his life, must therefore be false, if by its application, it excludes any other religion or belief system.

Even scientists and cosmologists now accept the possibility that everything may be connected by one interconnected sub-atomic *membrane*. Scientists are currently seeking to explain the very essence of the universe's creation though the existence of parallel universes woven inside our own. Having never seen a parallel universe I have difficulty reconciling such a hypothesis, but if you replace that membrane with the concept of a universal force, it is remarkable how science and the existence of God comes close to being proven by mathematical formulae.

The "*God in you and everything that exists*" definition of God is a pretty wide ranging and all encompassing definition. This might at first appear a bitter pill to swallow when confronted with a history of fundamentalist belief in a God system, built upon blind faith and dogmatic interpretation of old texts. None the less it bears the unmistakable hallmark of truth to the open and inquiring mind. The fact that you have obtained this book confirms that you have a mind that is looking for the truth.

It is possible to accept blind faith as an acceptable belief system when you are a child. When you are a child you know no better and trust your parents or guardians, who bring you up, to provide you with a sound and reliable education. Much of this is based upon example. Society as a whole needs rules and good example to provide the secure basis upon which it can sustain itself. In consequence the Bible – one of the great teaching books of all time – provided the Ten Commandments as a rule of law upon which early society could be formed. These rules eventually contributed to the multitude of laws, which now are spread far and wide.

In the same way that society moves forward and the consciousness of humanity rises – so a child moves forward to become an adult. As an adult many of the things that you accepted as a child are challenged and you form a new view, or a new opinion, based upon your own experiences. You may question your parents belief system and you may choose a different way of life. This is natural progression and, whilst respecting one's parents view, it is quite normal to develop your own opinions upon aspects of life which previously as a child you had never considered before. You do this because you have learnt to use your own experience and intellect to make decisions for yourself. You have learnt through those things that happen to you and you follow your own instinct.

As you become older you start to communicate with your inner voice. As a child this inner voice provides you with imagination with which you can create your own imaginary world in which to play. Later that same voice is able to have logical and extended internal discussions with you, completely protected from the outside world. Later that same voice can direct you into new areas of life experience. This voice is known to you as "*me*" or "*I*" in normal conversation, as you need a term to understand how this "*thinking process*" occurs. Later you will realise that there are occasions when that same voice inside your head directs you to perform certain deeds such as *"Why don't **you** do this or that"* – directing you in a specific manner that the intelligence seeks you to behave. When you recognise this fact without blindly following your own ego then you have made your first link to understanding the way the Divine Spirit works – and I shall deal with this later.

It is clear to any thinking person that the concept of God sitting on high in "*heaven*" is seriously flawed. This concept does not fit the real world we live in today. A world where thoughts can travel across the planet at the speed of light via the Internet, radio or television. Blind faith that sends men to their deaths for martyrdom or upon crusades in furtherance of holy wars cannot be justified by a higher consciousness. This is not to say that those who believe in a God or "*heaven*" in such a fashion are wrong – since it is within their own mind to allow God to manifest in this way.

In a philosophical sense the people who cannot see beyond this position are like children who have not yet grown up, who keep repeating the mistakes of their parents. They cannot be blamed for this – we should feel sorry for them. Blind faith is no longer acceptable to the raised consciousness. You and I are no longer living in the Dark Ages or beyond, where people are uneducated and ignorant. The issue is one of seeking the fundamental truth that allows us to understand who we are and what our relationship is with our maker. This will fulfil the function of providing the higher consciousness with the answer. We must now seek this truth to what our function is. Understanding our function will free us from the past and unlock our true potential to become advanced human souls.

With this understanding you will see that this book of life works for all religions. In seeking to understand this I will bring you to understand that whilst religion serves its purpose, as one of the moral building blocks of humanity, a time comes when the way you conduct your life, and the way that you live in balance with nature and your fellow man, is more important than the religious belief that brought you to that place. When the sun rises and the shadows are gone you can see clearly, because the shadow that was in your heart has been replaced by the light of day with which you can see the truth.

You can only be at one with your God when there is perfect understanding and perfect respect. In order to achieve that you must be able to communicate with that Divine Spirit and *know* its existence – rather than be told by a teacher. Knowing is the experience rather than the result of teaching by religious organisations or even this book. Knowing can come from learning from others, or it can come directly from the spirit in the form of a "Gnostic experience" (from the Latin *gnosis* meaning knowledge) In understanding who you are you will know the existence of the Divine and experience the oneness of everlasting life. Once you stand at the threshold of recognition of who you really are, and what your destiny is, you will cast off the past and move forward to that new future that you know deep inside awaits you.

This does not mean that in order to understand who you are or why you are here you also need to abandon your God or current belief system. This philosophy accommodates all religions, since it recognises that the child needs a mechanism to understand what is too complicated for a child to know. However when the child grows up it is their decision how to deal or adapt their previously held beliefs to accommodate what they now know to be true. We do not abandon our parents because we have learnt something that our parents did not know.

In this book I show you the way to conduct your life and the way to communicate with the Divine Spirit in your daily life. This will lead you to know who you are and why you are here. When this is done and you have experienced that contact you will no longer need those structures you used as a child. The one and only God has an infinite number of names, but for the sake of consistency in this document we shall call this element of our new life The Divine Spirit.

The Oceanist

In order to better understand the concept of the Divine Spirit let us imagine an ocean covering the bedrock that we call the Universe. In most places it is deep and bottomless and covers everything. There is a beach somewhere in this ocean, which might represent this small place which we call earth. On that beach are billions and billions of grains of sand that equate to all the individual souls that exist.

These souls, like the ocean that surrounds them cannot die, because they are all made from an energy form. Science has shown us that energy can change form, but cannot be destroyed. The same rules of science underpin the Divine Spirit and the human spirit. God can after all not exist except within the rules that have been created for all existence. Hence these grains of sand, whilst separate from the bedrock and the sea of the Divine Spirit, are in truth made from the same material, but are in a different form.

If you can accept that the basic building blocks of the Universe are atoms or energy, then the understanding that we are all made from the same material can equally apply to the existence of the Divine. The Divine can be shown to manifest itself as an intelligence, why should we assume that such an intelligence does not exist under the same or similar rules as everything else? It would be foolish to attribute other rules that have never been demonstrated by science or intellect to be true.

These grains of sand (souls) have a coat of moisture that causes them to stick together. This moisture represents each life of the grain, holding it in position, yet effected by the interaction of the sea. Each grain interacts with those close by and also with the sea, since it is within the power of the sea to move those grains if it wishes. The sand in its basic form is part of the underlying bedrock. Presented another way the bedrock is an inherent part of the sea, because the sea cannot exist unless it rests upon this base. Whilst you may not be able to see the bedrock it is part of the sea. It is created out of precipitation from the elements that make the sea, in a continuous cycle of creation and reabsorbtion.

The souls that exist on this planet can no more die than the atoms of the grains of sand that frequent our philosophical beach can be destroyed. They can only change form as they slowly return to the sea and return to their constituent elements. As the millennia pass new bedrock is formed from precipitation from the sea. Old grains dissolve to be recycled and in turn become new bedrock in the course of time.

In this way life forms out of the global ocean of the Divine Spirit. Individual souls, whilst separate from the Divine Spirit, are like the sand grains which pass their time on the beach of life - until they have reached their time to return to the sea. Returning does not happen in one or even many lives, but only when they have achieved a level of understanding which will allow them to make the transition back to pure spirit.

The sea on the other hand exists as a universal force, ever present, able to shape and move the beach as it wishes. Some grains sit at the back of the beach immovably stuck in position through their own lack of understanding. Others wash through the surf every hour of every day in a constant state of flux.

Each tide, like life, brings new experiences and new relationships. Those who are on the beach may experience thousands of tides, but never see it move - because every movement is too small in itself to be recognised. In the same way each element of life appears to have no impact upon humanity as a whole. Every day appears to pass without change - yet life too changes every day in a smallest way. Every experience of every soul, in all existence, makes up the total of the experience of the Divine Spirit.

This analogy of a beach with sand and the sea with underlying bedrock and tide of life opens the door to understanding the interchangeable nature of the human and Divine Spirit. It offers a simplistic understanding of how souls exist separately, but united with God as one. The Divine Spirit is not therefore the atoms themselves, as science would seek to explain the power of the human spirit, but the force that occupies the space between those atoms, as well as the space inside them. A force that like gravity operates everywhere, is immensely powerful, but unable to be seen except by its effect. A force that cannot be measured at this time, yet can be shown to exist through the communication with your inner voice.

Who can deny that there is something called a life-force. Who can deny that this life-force can implement its will at an individual and collective level? It is possible that you have not experienced this force yourself in your daily life at a personal level. This book will change that if you follow its example.

The analogy of how life is like the sea and the beach helps explain the mystery of reincarnation to those with inquiring minds who cannot understand how reincarnation can be possible. Science will tell us that each year more grains of sand exist upon this beach, but does not take into account the fundamental nature of what those "*grains of sand*" are made from. Once it is understood that the force that you call life, and the force that we call the Divine Spirit, are one and the same, then the picture can be drawn into focus. There is no limit to the number of grains when the two are interchangeable

In many respect the early Jewish understood this in a conceptual manner by applying the analogy of God holding a bucket filled with souls. God issued the souls from the bucket until the bucket was empty and then recalled the souls so that he could issue them again. Much of those early philosophical teachings have now been lost in the dogma of commercialised religion. This analogy is a direct reference to reincarnation, which runs contrary to the idea of going to heaven, even though it has a common sense ring to it. Even the least educated knows you cannot every year have more and more souls populating the same space.

The number of souls able to exist is limitless, since the transfer from one form to another within the Divine Spirit's total capacity is limitless. Our freedom to exist as one of those grains of sand has no effect upon either the sea or the bedrock in the universal allocation of spirit. The soul is not replaced when the new tide of life comes, but simply takes a new outer coat of moisture on the beach. The fact that more or less grains exist on the beach this year than last is an expression of the Divine will. Should the Divine wish to return all souls to the sea and remove the beach completely, then no act of man could change this, as the sea exerts its own will.

The logical conclusion of these observations is that when you cease to exist as a separate spiritual entity you do not die. This is because those basic elements from which you are formed cannot be lost, any more than the energy that is released from the split of an atom. There is good scientific reason to know that energy – no matter what form it exists cannot be destroyed. It should therefore come as no surprise to understand that your soul operates under the same rules. The concept of reincarnation is therefore nothing more than an understanding of the physics that bind every atom in our bodies. Reincarnation is not a control mechanism for higher or lower life forms to explain why some are more important than others. It shows we are all in the same bucket and interchangeable.

The above analogy helps to provide an understanding of what I might call the global picture of how we and the Divine Spirit are one and the same. This force, which is in everything, does not on the face of it appear to function as one entity. We can observe humans in conflict with one and other, as well as operating through a host of different belief systems. Each soul appears to have its own will and is able to operate completely independently of any Divine control structure.

As well as this we can see that many souls deny the existence of the Divine because they fail to understand or remember who they really are.

Those who fail to see the Divine Spirit either in themselves or the world around them have lost touch with their maker. They have forgotten who they really are and where they come from. The Divine Spirit flows through our lives in daily contact with us all and manifests in all the great experiences of life, from the greatness of nature, music and art, to the every day human experience. However many humans have now lost touch with themselves and their God as a result of failing to hear the voice that is there to guide them.

They do not hear their voice because they have not yet tuned their mind to the processes that make them do what they need to do. They live in a world where the need for God has diminished and have as a result they have put their "*faith*" in the things and products of a consumer society. In so doing they have turn their back upon God. It is clear to any thinking person that as a result of this the faith that is required by the major religions no longer serves the needs of a modern well-educated thinking person.

These people represent the mass of humanity currently deserting the churches in the western world, seeking a new truth. Some turn to consumerism, some turn to cults, whilst the great majority have come to turn away from the Divine in the worship of money above all things. The decision to turn away from God has not been made consciously, but out of a state of ignorance. This is because those new gods appear to be far more influential than the Divine Spirit ever could be in this modern world.

This state of ignorance cannot be changed by external events, but can only be changed through the understanding that comes with inner communication. Unlike teachings from ancient texts the new human can only experience the Divine through his own perceptions. Once awoken you can never go back. In consequence if there is an objective for this book it is to awaken that communication process in you.

In order to expand our understanding of how the Divine Spirit communicates in our daily life we must look closer at how it works. We need to look carefully at the development and delivery of thought processes; for this we need to examine the workings of the mind. The sand and the sea explanation of how life exists in relation to God helps explain the many references to "*eternal life*" in the Bible, as taught by Christ and all the great prophets. These prophets were enlightened souls who bought us the sparks of knowledge needed to light the flames that move human consciousness forward. Each analogy was appropriate for its time – a new understanding is now needed that explains these fundamental issues in a scientifically credible way. Blind faith is no longer enough. It is now time to take the next step forward. The time is now right to know the Divine Spirit for what it is. Those who understand this way of explaining how the Divine Spirit operates would call themselves an "*Oceanist*". *An Oceanist* is someone who understands how the Divine Spirit works as an analogy of the inter-action of the sand and the sea on the beach of life.

The Deception of the Mind

The mechanism used to communicate between the Divine Spirit and the human entity in daily life is called the mind. It is not as many would believe located in the brain. The mind occupies our whole being and operates at a level which science is currently unable to measure.

This is not unusual because science is not the master of the Universe that it would like to make itself out to be. Science seeks to explain everything in terms of what it has recently experienced. In consequence science understands that a brain is a computer – simply because it cannot understand it as anything else. Nevertheless men of science have sought to explain the brain as the centre of existence, whilst in the past others thought it may be in the heart.

There is good reason for this, because the heart appears to be the centre of feeling. Do you not feel love through the heart? Do you not feel the cutting of the etheric chords of death through the heart? All those who have lost a loved one must know this to be true – you do not feel the pain of death of a loved one in the brain – you feel that pain more strongly in your chest, where your heart is located.

Each age can find a different analogy to suit its time and now as man moves forward we seek to understand the mind in a way that men 500 years ago could never conceive. Could Galileo have conceived of thoughts being able to travel around the planet the way they do today? Could Newton have understood what satellite television is?

The mind, as opposed to the brain, is that part of you which is timeless and connected to your soul. It does not sleep, but is in constant communication with every aspect of your existence, as well as all the bodily functions that you need to exist. The mind is a force that is made from exactly the same material as the Divine Spirit. If the brain is the computer then the mind is *the hands on the keyboard*. Whilst the computer can carry out the basic functions it is the mind that directs the computer and directs your life.

The mind unlike the brain is not confined to the body. This is probably the most important discovery that you will ever possibly make, if you take the trouble to train yourself. The mind exists in and around our body and can best be described as like an electric field of energy. It appears to exist as if in a very thin transparent shell that separates our existence from the Divine.

The mind appears to have seven energy levels, which are well known to psychics. These energy levels start at the lowest vibrations, being the physical level at which objects exist and rise through the seven levels to the highest Divine level. It is not necessary for me to go into great detail here - because there are many thousands of books devoted to the study of the human psychic existence. Should you wish to further your knowledge in these areas it is recommended that you follow your inner voice on which books to read and which to abandon.

It is not difficult to have an out of body experience. The effect of which can have immensely beneficial aspects in understanding the nature of your existence.

The mind operates at many different levels, but is recognisable to you during your daily life in the form of your inner voice. It manifests itself as the voice which appears to be located in your head. This voice speaks for you and is the result of your learning process through life. We have discussed this briefly in the earlier chapter. It speaks with the expression "*I*" in the form "*I will do this*", "*I will do that*" and by numerous logical functions whereby the thought process evaluates decisions upon the basis of "*If I do this – then that will happen or I will do that*".

This voice I call the "*I voice*" because I can hear it all the time and I recognise it as "*me*" – the me that I understand to be the person that I am.

However the mind is not isolated on its own - but like the material from which it is made is connected to the Divine Spirit through a communication system. Whilst the mind is operating within a very thin shell that surrounds us it is incredibly complicated. It also communicates through this shell to the rest of the force in which it operates.

In this way we are not spiritually separated from the Divine Spirit but part of it. Indeed the greater Divine Spirit can communicate directly with all of us and does so every day. It does this through a deception, which most people fail to recognise. This deception is very simple, but able to fool those who have never looked. It speaks with their own voice – fooling them to believe that it came through their normal thought process.

In this way the Divine Spirit is able to implement its will through you and all humanity. In this way it is not possible for you to avoid the will of the Divine Spirit and in this way human existence is shaped. We are effectively all connected to the giant mainframe computer of the Divine Spirit. We operate our own personal computers, ignorant of the fact that all the other entities through which we react are part of the same network. Everyone has the same hands in ultimate control on their keyboard too.

We operate in ignorance of the guide that keeps us on a global course and this is a course that is often referred to as The Divine Plan. Whilst we may seek our own destiny free of interference we cannot escape the destiny of the Divine Plan. This is why people such as Nostradamus and the thirteenth century Indian prophets could see a thousand years into the future with some certainty. Prophesy, which we shall deal with later, confirms that the Divine Will is inescapable.

Recent scientific studies of how the brain works have shown that thought processes in the brain appear to start before it is possible for the body to know that a reaction is required. These observations confirm the existence of the divine nature and confirms the "*hands on the keyboard*" for those who care to look.

Whilst the mind is therefore able to operate under the guise of free will this is because nothing is ever forced upon it by the Divine Spirit. The Divine Spirit does not need to force any issue because it is neutral and cannot break its own laws. It communicates with you in your own voice, requesting that you should do something that is required. It speaks to you all the time and it is up to you to recognise this voice, because it always speaks to you and addresses you using what I shall call the "*you voice*". It sounds like the "*I voice*" but speaks to you in a different way. This is explained by reference to the following examples of thought processes "*Why don't you go and see your sister today?*", "*You shouldn't do that because...*", "*You could do well if you did that*" etc etc.

Indeed the most interesting aspect of this deception, which we perpetrate upon ourselves, is that even when trained to know the difference it is often impossible to separate the two voices easily in daily life. One originating within you and the other being directed to you. None the less one voice operates your own sphere of experience and the other operates in the total sphere of experience. It is therefore necessary, as a human being in a higher state of consciousness, to seek to recognise which is which in daily life. To recognise the communication process allows you to understand the part you play and allows you to work in harmony with the will of the Divine Spirit.

This is the way that the world has been run since the beginning of the time of men. Each man is offered free will in each life within the confines of the direct communication process of the "*you voice*". No man is forced to listen to that voice and frequently ignores it or opposes it. Opposition to that will simply mean that you have chosen poorly and are unlikely to succeed, simply because the communication process allows another route to the chosen objective to be taken by the Divine Spirit.

Put in simplistic terms the voice goes another route, using its will to move men in the giant chess game of life. It is because men have this internal communication system that there is no need ever for the Divine Spirit to materialise in human form. It is already in human form in every person who has existed and still exists. Indeed the Divine will does not stop at humans, but of course extends to planets, stars and all elements of the Universe - everything.

In many respects the ancient Greeks understood how men were moved by the gods to do the will that the gods expected of them. Now we see things differently, but the effect of how the world moves can be seen to be the same under one Divine Spirit.

Life on this planet appears to be an experiment in separateness where the Divine Spirit has chosen to express itself in human form. It is therefore easier to understand the trials and tribulations of each life once we understand that we are simply an extension of its own self - separated by that filter around our being.

Once this is understood we no longer see God as being on our side in war, because God is on both sides in equal measure. The concept of death is simply a means to another life and God is never responsible for human suffering, because it is men that implement suffering. The Divine Spirit seeks to guide us daily and it is up to us either to listen or choose another path. Those who choose the Divine Path choose a life in tune with their maker and a life that is designed to make you happy. Those who choose their own path choose their own cause and effect.

There is no retribution from on high and there certainly is no hell because, hell and heaven are the same thing – the Divine experience. There is only learning and the effect of the things that we do. At the same time no man can escape the Divine Will because we all are part of that process.

The first step to being able to understand who you are and to recognise your own divinity is to hear your maker though your own "*you voice*". Meditation is the time honoured best method of learning how to separate the two voices. Meditation is not an easy path, but one you are almost certainly going to face at some stage in your path to enlightenment. The sooner you start the wiser and greater a human being you will become.

Meditation

The gateway to the Divine is the act of meditation. This has been known for ten thousand years in the Eastern countries, where prophets such as Buddha have opened the door to understanding of who we are. Those who practice the belief systems of both the Buddhist and Hindu religions should have little difficulty understanding the concepts written in this book. If there is any religion which has the hallmark of truth, then it is probably the Hindu belief system above all others. This recognises the basic nature of eternal life, through reincarnation and the nature of the Divine Spirit, through its inter-action with men and nature.

In the West the Hindu belief in gods in the form of statues and idols is not generally understood. This is because the West has been heavily influenced by Christian dogma. This teaches that the worship of idols is a sin – stemming from the biblical story of the Israelites flight from Egypt, where they worship a golden calf. The proliferation of statues in temples of Hindu culture has therefore been misunderstood by casual observers, who have failed to look deeper than they should.

The Hindu already understands that the Divine Spirit is in everything and that includes all men, as well as nature. In many ways this is advanced thinking compared to Western belief in a God on high, who sits on a throne in Heaven. A place that there is no evidence for whatsoever in the human experience. The development of the Hindu god is a way of expressing the many faces of the Divine Spirit. It is not an attempt to worship many gods, as some in the West have been led to believe. Each god is an expression of the Divine Spirit in a way that men have understood the actions of the Divine Spirit, since men first walked upon the planet.

The Hindu sees the Divine Spirit in the form of storms and lightening which may be expressed as one god, whilst the Divine in the form of love comes in the form of another. Each god is an embodiment of the understanding of one aspect of the Divine Spirit, as a united entity guiding us all through life. In consequence the statues are themselves of no significance, as the worship applied to them is not upon the statue itself, but the concept of the manifestation of the Divine Spirit in that particular form. Hindus do not therefore need either temples, priests or statues, because the Divine Spirit is everywhere in their life. The statues simply form a focus upon which the mind can visualise the otherwise impossible visualisation.

It is no surprise to find that the Hindu culture originated in the Indus Valley which runs into Kashmir, Pakistan and Afghanistan. The very word Hindu being a derivative of Indus – a river that brings life to that region. That same culture being the birth place of humanity.

The Eastern religions teach that each life is a learning course that leads us towards enlightenment. Enlightenment is simply the same as the return to pure spirit that we all achieve in the course of time and learning. This is the same as expressed through the sea and beach analogy, where each grain of sand is returned to the sea when the time comes.

The Eastern religions also teach that as each life passes we experience events, which not surprisingly operate under the basic rules of the universe - such as *cause and effect*. This too has a basis in science, once the rules of the universe are understood and we remember who we are. These rules are as solid as the science we learn at school. Once you become aware that life does not end at death then there is no reason to doubt that every cause should not create an effect. We all know that even in outer space every action has an equal and opposite reaction, which can be measured by science. So too in life every action is measured and has an effect. Sometimes the effect is immediate and sometimes it cannot be seen at all. The spiritual record created in this way carries with you through life and death into each following life. It builds into a record which Eastern sages call *karma*.

Once you become aware of your own immortality karma plays an important control upon advanced human beings, because you know that death is not the end of everything. Whilst in a state of ignorance it was assumed that death freed you from responsibility for your actions. When awakened to the true nature of the universe it doesn't take long to realise that eternal life also means eternal accountability. Death no longer provides the escape that you once believed in. Now every action has a value that goes beyond death.

This does not mean that as a result of living a life of greed that you will return to the next life as a pet dog. The interplay of karma and the human spirit is far more sophisticated than that. It may mean that a person who abuses another may return in the next life to be abused in a similar or worse way by the very spirit they abused. It may mean that a person who lives a life of greed and glutton may spend the next in poverty and famine – as many do. Karmic bonds are created in every life that tie us to people and places that transcend time. These bonds cannot be broken until such time as the karmic debt is repaid. Karma is absolute and unforgiving, because its actions fall upon those responsible for their action. Karma cannot be excused or passed to a third party.

Cause and effect operates as the judge and jury of all men's actions, since karma operates through eternal life and cannot be escaped any more than the spirits of people from the past can be destroyed. In consequence those who have lived before are still with us today. They have either learnt from their past mistakes, or continue to make the same ones until such time as they can move on. Great souls good and bad do not die, but return to continue their destiny, as do you. Souls tend to travel through life together, returning to the places they have occupied in previous lives and being attracted to relationships they have built previously. This is often explained as déja-vu by those who are not familiar with their own history.

Bonds form between people at the etheric level of our being. The etheric level is a physical level, which is one of the seven levels of existence. The etheric level is like an electronic network communications system, which maintains structure to your physical body, but also communicates with others at a subconscious level. It is not usual to be able to see this level of activity but it can be seen when your consciousness rises beyond a certain point. It is recognised by psychics under the generic name of the *Aura.* Seeing the aura is a first step along the road of understanding the wonder of your mind and can be achieved relatively quickly. To see something that we all possess for the first time opens the mind to the understanding that other things that you may have read about could also exist to your perception, should you be prepared to devote your time to it's development.

The etheric level can form bonds between lovers, family, friends and places, which if broken by death or physical parting can create real pain in those who experience it. This pain is emotional, because it communicates at a higher level than normal pain. Unlike normal pain it is felt in the heart and chest at the point where these communications processes occur. None can deny the pain of the death of a loved one is a real pain. Science is only just starting to understand the underlying spiritual nature of what makes man tick. The advanced soul instinctively knows that there is much that science cannot yet explain and probably never will.

The fact that you are questioning your life and are reading this book is a sign that you are probably unable to reconcile all elements of your philosophical belief system. A true philosophical belief system must be able to explain why more people exist every year and how reincarnation operates in this environment. A true belief system must also explain why people die of famine and plague every year. It must explain why children die in childbirth. It must answer the person who has lost a loved one and the person who suffers pain, either emotional or physical. A true philosophy of life will answer all unasked questions as well. These unasked questions are the ones that undermine Western religious teachings, but people are often too afraid to ask.

Why for instance doesn't anyone ask the Catholic Church to explain how more and more people each year fit into heaven? Will I meet cavemen in heaven? If everyone is saved by the Son of God where is Hell? Surely it's not needed any more? Why should I believe in something that I have no experience of? Why doesn't anyone ask the Christians why the gospels tell us that if we believe in God we shall have "*everlasting life*" (John 3.36). Isn't that telling us that if we believe in the true God we shall understand that we live for ever? Since when was the expression "*everlasting life*" meant to be "*heaven*". If Jesus and the disciples had meant heaven they would have said it – John referred eight times to "*everlasting life*" in Jesus' teachings. Isn't that telling us that reincarnation was actively promoted by the great Christian teachers, but has been misrepresented for two thousand years?

A true understanding of life must be able to answer all questions without contradiction and not be exclusive in what evidence it seeks to allow. A true belief system is one that accommodates the failings of all religions, by recognising their failings and providing the answer to the unanswered questions.

If heaven exists then the nature of eternal life must mean that proof of heaven must exist for men to wisely believe in such a thing. Equally well, for men to believe in hell then proof of hell must also exist. We no longer live in the fourteenth century where it was sufficient to be told by someone who could read and write that "*it is so*". Nowadays you can read and write and have access to a hundred thousand times more information. Information that has been checked, verified and inspected by humanity over many centuries. Tell me – is it logical to accept the dogma of heaven and hell upon the word of a priest? Show me a priest who has more faith now that one a thousand years ago? Have we, as humanity, really learnt nothing in the last thousand years?

Proof of reincarnation on the other hand is much easier to find than many would believe. It is easy to find children who remember past life experiences in India and in countries that understand the true nature of our existence. People who remember who they were in a previous life and more often than not still carry physical scars from past life experiences.

Western intellectuals have sneered at Eastern mystics since the Victorian colonisation of India in the belief that the "*good book*" that they carried, and an inherent belief in science was greater than any truth held by native hearts. The Victorians had a lot to answer for, unaware that their ancestors wore animal skins when the Eastern cultures were at their greatest. Victorians even changed maps – removing biblical name places from maps of Kashmir in the misguided belief that Abraham could never have been a native – even though the evidence of their own bible pointed to the north-east of India as the birthplace of humanity.

In order for you to find the answer to what you are looking for, and know deep inside you it is there, you must first look inside yourself. You do not need to consult anyone else for his or her opinion, you should be warned that it is dangerous to do so.

You have everything you need to know the absolute truth about yourself. All you have to do is look inside. This is the most difficult task for many, because most people have not been trained in the art of looking. Meditation is the doorway to a higher consciousness, because it allows you to open the doorway to communicate with your inner voice – the real you waiting to welcome you to a new world.

The art of communication is the ability which meditation provides to allow you to turn off what I have referred to previously as the "*I voice*". Many philosophers call this the ego, because it represents the will of the human who has grown up from birth. It is better explained by seeing humans as having two halves of their existence. There is the side of our existence that is timeless, which we bring with us from our previous lives. We call this the soul, as it is connected to the Divine Spirit, even if we cannot usually directly communicate with it. There is the other side, which starts at birth and is based upon the experiences of this life. This is called the ego and manifests itself through the "*I voice*."

The "*I voice*" learns quickly that it is able to direct your life and assimilates knowledge. It can compute actions and estimate responses. It communicates throughout life with the "*you voice*" as we have discussed earlier and dominates your thought processes.

The act of meditation is a control system that teaches you how to turn off the "*I voice*" to allow you to communicate with your "*you voice*". This in turn allows you to communicate at the deepest level of your existence directly with the Divine

Spirit. When I say this I do not mean that you communicate in an esoteric way like a one way prayer with no-one listening. I mean real communication, with a voice that is real, knows you completely and from which nothing can be hidden. A voice that responds to your needs and guides you through life.

When you do this it has an amazing effect upon you and your life. You can spend your whole life repeating words out of a book, parrot fashion, singing praise to your God. You can make statements of faith until your last dying breath. Most of these you know deep inside are repeated more like an insurance policy, than any knowledge of truth. Selling insurance for your spirit has been the plague of the churches for the last thousand years – the time has come to recognise that you don't need insurance when you experience truth. Experience is the only truth. Nothing I say will convince you until the day comes when you hear that voice – and you know with whom you are communicating. This is an awe inspiring and life changing experience.

The truth is that you do not need to learn from outside. Everything you need is already there inside you waiting to be remembered. Once remembered your life will change in a way that I cannot explain. You will find the real world. You will know who you are and you will be freed from ten thousand years of history. You will hear with your own ears and there will be no-one else to deflect you from the true understanding of what your life is about and why you are here.

All that stands in your way is the constant chatter of the voice that has grown with you since birth. Training to silence that voice will allow the voice of the Divine Spirit to communicate directly with you through your "*you voice*" in a controlled and life enhancing way.

You will learn to hear your "*you voice*" in the daily grind of life. You will learn to trust it completely and as a result your life will fulfil itself. God will be with you in a way that has never been before. More importantly you will be happy. This is happiness born out of the satisfaction of spiritual need, as opposed to physical need – something that is so deep inside you that you should not need anything else to feed your soul - because you will know who you are and why you are here.

Meditation leads to remembering who you are. It releases the memories of past lives and experiences. These may come as dreams or visions, which you will remember. Remembering does not come quickly, but does come – opening the door to understanding who you really are and who you have been.

Meditation is not the providence of priests, prophets and the elite. It belongs to everyone and does not even need to be taught in a specific manner. Those who make a living from selling meditation courses and New Age philosophies will not appreciate what I have to say. Every person can find their own method of meditation in a way that suits them best. In my case I learnt to meditate by accident, because the time had come in my spiritual growth to do what was needed. It came to me at a time of crisis, but will come to you either when you need to do it, or when you are right to make the transition to move towards being an advanced human being.

There is no great Divine Plan which says you should meditate in one particular way. I needed to commute two hours to work every day upon a train. I used to leave quite early in the morning and found that if I adopted a favourite posture and closed my eyes I would drift into sleep. The rhythmic sound of the track and the act of getting into the train every morning at the same time set the scene for what would follow. Meditation grows stronger by the ritual of repeated actions.

I expect that it was the regular stopping of the train as it passed through the commuter belt that kept bringing me back to consciousness. Then one day I realised that I was communicating with someone or something. Each time I came back to consciousness I found I could at first remember a snatch of a discussion. A few words here and there.

At first I was not sure what was going on. I decided to learn more about what was happening to me and read a number of books upon psychic experiences, psychic growth and the art of meditation. They taught me to practice at home closing my mind to the constant chatter of my own ego. I would lie in bed at night and close down my body, using a well known close down method. This took the form of telling each part of the body in turn to close down, starting at the feet and working up the body.

This is easy – especially in bed - but of course very difficult to maintain, because the body likes to go to sleep when given the opportunity. Perseverance wins through and provided you persevere you too will achieve your goal.

Then I learnt with practice to close down the chattering voice in my head. This is undoubtedly the most difficult exercise. Some seek to do this through rhythmic chanting. The use of a rhythmic chant has the same effect – it excludes the mind from being able to create thought processed to divert you. In so doing it is possible to keep that chattering voice at bay over longer and longer periods.

The first thing to take on board is that successful meditation is best adopted in the form of a ritual. At first you may only be successful for a few seconds or minutes if you are lucky. However the daily observance of the same ritual appears to build strength of mind that allows the quietening effect to take place.

I no longer commute and have replaced the ritual of getting on the train with the ritual of a bath every day. I find this the best way to meditate in a busy household. It fulfils the requirements that make success that much easier to achieve. Bathing in the morning also has the advantage of not being overwhelmed by a tired body pushing you into sleep – which is all too easy.

The elements that contribute towards successful meditation are firstly a place that you feel safe in and will not be disturbed – a bathroom is good for this because it can be locked. A bedroom may be equally suitable. The next element is doing your meditation exercises on a regular daily basis. This adds weight to what you are doing, as the act of meditation is done in a ritualistic way. The effect is for the act itself to pass a message to the subconscious that puts you quickly into the frame of mind required to let go of the bonds that bind your mind to the physical. Meditation is the training of the mind and therefore the exercise's primary aim is to free your mind from the awareness of either your body or the chattering voice within.

As time passes you will find that by adopting a ritualistic approach to meditation the act of going to your place of meditation at a specific time of day will advance the meditation process. Instead of needing to adopt exercises to empty the mind the act itself of getting into the bath, or lying in the same bed, or chair in a specific manner is enough to put you into a deep state of consciousness. A state where your mind frees itself from your body very quickly.

To begin with it is enough simply to instruct the voice that creeps into your head to stop. That is the only thing you need to do. When it starts up again remind it to go away until it is required.

Do this for two minutes by organising yourself so that you can achieve that. It sounds easy but believe me it is not. Then the art is to lengthen the time to five minutes. That is five minutes without any thought process. The total absence of logical thoughts and an empty head.

The amount of time this takes will depend upon you. Some people may achieve this in a month and some may never achieve it if they are not ready. The rewards to control of the mind are far greater than you can imagine, as a point will come when you will hear your "*you voice*". For many this will be the first time and can be life-changing.

The object of these exercises is to close the active mind. If you are not meditating in a bath then it is best to wear clothing that will not constrict. In order to close the mind you need to be unaware of your clothing or surroundings. However bearing in mind that any commuter can use the time to meditate, as I did, there are no rules that apply to everyone. Every person has to find their own way.

In my case I close my mind by taking the conscious decision not to engage in thought. It took me nearly six months practice before the big break came. I had read about the theory in a number of books, but nothing prepared me for the change when it came.

When you first start meditation it is a hard grind with a goal that isn't well defined, because you do not know what it is that you can achieve. You really need to be dedicated and you need to persevere. Nothing happens quickly. I simply repeated the process of doing what I did in the train, but in the far more comfortable bathroom scenario. I follow the same procedure every day. Starting by thanking the Divine Spirit for another day in this life. I close my eyes and tell myself not to think. Which is fine until about two seconds later when the thought processes take over. Which is when I realise about five minutes later that I am meant to be meditating.

You have to remember that you are in charge of your body and mind. This means that you have to tell that voice to be quiet. You have to be able to hear yourself and you can only do that when the voice is quiet. Meditation is the doorway to your existence. If you are ready to walk through it you will find a welcome there that you would never have believed possible.

I believe that it is a natural activity for the advanced soul to meditate. Meditation produces balance in our lives and allows our inner guide to direct us to the advancement of our own lives and humanity generally. Meditation should never be a forced activity, as it can only operate under free will. Meditation brings every one of us closer to the Divine Spirit and in so doing brings us closer to understanding the true concept of Love.

Love

Love is the greatest force in the universe and a form of the Divine Spirit. It is by its very nature intangible, since no man can measure or weigh love. It is a manifestation of the human spirit and hence grows or diminishes out of life experience. There is only love that transcends life – since love exists as an experience of the Divine. As each life passes the only value that is carried forward from life to life is the eternal experience of love. Love is the reason we exist, love encapsulates the essence of both the Divine and human experience as one.

Our reason to exist is to make love greater and in so doing to bring ourselves nearer the Divine in each life experience. Hence the ultimate goal of all life is to return to the Divine in the experience of total love.

This is understood by Buddhists as the "*path to enlightenment*", whilst the same concept is portrayed as "*returning to the Father*" in Christian texts. In essence both are correct but applying different analogies. Each faith has taken the literal word of their teacher and used this to implement an understanding that has been embellished by generation after generation of religious doctrine. Strip away this doctrine, study the original texts and all true religions address the same fundamentals garnished in different interpretations. Strip away these interpretations and you are left with one simple message that all faiths can accept – there is only one God and this God manifests itself through Love.

Whether God wears a Christian, Hindu or Muslim hat is of no consequence to those who have freed themselves of religious dogma – since visualisation of God's existence in human form is only necessary when society and human existence is in a primeval state. That lower state of consciousness has suited humanity's existence since man first appeared on the planet. That primeval state is now coming to an end. Human consciousness is rising above the threshold of need – the need to know God in the human form.

Love is of course another word for "*good*" since the application of Love produces good - which in turn makes the Divine Spirit greater. The measure of every day's existence can be obtained by how much good you have been able to achieve each day, week, month or life.

The human experience called hate can therefore be better understood as the absence of love - materialising as one of the negative forces in life. Love produces positive forces, with hate producing the opposite effect. A man who hates his neighbour is experiencing absence of love – which materialises in his own anger. This will also appear in life as a negative force, which can often be felt both at spiritual as well as physical level. Many aspects of ill health are caused by carried forward psychic elements from past life experiences. These can only be removed by dealing with the core problems - hence the tremendous growth in past-life regression treatment, as well as many new science treatments based upon the reinstatement of balance. No matter how you seek to deal with these issues past life problems are eventually dealt with under the rules of karma, through cause and effect – they are not avoidable.

Evil is therefore another way of explaining the absence of good or love. Since we are part of the Divine Spirit we cannot create evil any more than an all loving God could create evil. Evil does not really exist, except in the minds of those who seek to indoctrinate you with their religious beliefs – a fear mechanism used to inspire you to feel guilt – one of their many control methods. Evil is simply an expression of understanding at a certain point in time, taken in the holistic sense. Evil is better understood as your own belief system endeavouring to explain what appears to be illogical.

This is of course very difficult to get your head around when your whole life has been bought up to believe in "*good*" and "*evil*". However the raised consciousness does not seek to apportion blame, since the Divine Spirit does not blame anyone. In order for us to be able to understand this you cannot ultimately blame the Divine Spirit for any human action – no matter how "*evil*" this action may appear, according to your old way of thinking. Evil is better understood as the spiritual concept of *making mistakes* along life's chosen path.

In order to understand the terrible deeds committed in this world, it is necessary to take on board that every soul has a life path. That path starts at birth and continues through to death, when a new life path is chosen. Those who follow their life path stay in tune with themselves and their surroundings, experiencing harmony and well being. Their life is good and the experiences they draw upon take them forward, enjoying a balanced life full of love.

Your life path may not take you where you expect to go. As a child the way forward appears clear. Then as you grow up to be a teenager everything that was clear becomes complicated. Later life seems to have clarity again. None the less it can change without warning and a simple decision can thrust you into a different direction at will. Throughout life the road is full of decisions on which path to take. Follow your chosen path and you will be happy. Follow your ego without recourse to your inner instincts and you will experience the results of that decision as a negative force in your life. Those terrible deeds, which do not appear to be reconcilable, without the concept of *evil,* are understood to be the mistakes of men who fail to follow their chosen life path.

During life we learn from experience and listen to the inner voice that guides us. Some choose not to listen to that voice and this is a mistake – it is not evil because the Divine Spirit, which controls everything, cannot create evil. If evil could be created then the Divine Spirit itself would be evil – something that modern clerics omit from their zealous sermons.

When humans make mistakes they are not inherently evil. No soul can die – in consequence every soul that has ever existed is in existence today. Each soul carries it's Karmic record with it and in consequence hopes to learn from the mistakes of previous, as well as present lives.

In order to understand your own existence better it is not possible to ignore those fundamental questions that religions fail to answer. One of the most fundamental being the question "*if there is an all loving God why does God create evil*?" –

"*Why are there wars?*" – "*Why do children die in famines?*" to name but a few.

Only a true philosophy can accommodate the answer to these questions.

The answer to these and many other seemingly impossible questions is that the Divine Spirit is in and part of all people and all things. It does not create evil. Every person has free will within the parameters of the Divine Plan and manifests his own love or lack of love. Some show more love than others and some appear to exist without very much love at all. Yet none are made evil, as evil is simply the manifestation of little love. Such people rarely experience true values in life, as their lack of love brings them pain, as they move along their life path in conflict with their chosen path. This pain is a result of the life mistakes that drive them. None escape their karma, which accompanies them in this life, as well as those that follow. Almost without exception those who manifest such lack of love that they would be known as evil, inevitably bring upon themselves such karmic retribution, that they often terminate their own lives before their time would be due.

The true answer to those questions is therefore logical and persuasive to the advanced soul. God does and cannot create evil. God does not create wars and children do not die of famine because of God. Everything that we seek to blame God for is the direct result of men and no other reason.

At a fundamental level men are no different from animals or the mountains, planets or the stars in the sky. None are evil. A lion is not evil because it kills a zebra in order to live. A mountain is not evil because it kills ten thousand people when a volcano erupts, because of a fissure in the earth's surface. Each exists as an experience of the Divine with its own spiritual existence. Living under a volcano at a time when it explodes is a mistake. Walking where a lion hunts is also a mistake, which may cost the zebra its life. Making war is a mistake, which sometimes appears to have Divine influence. Children born with no food to eat is also a mistake – not one that carries blame, but one that explains why these matters are not the responsibility of the Divine. They are all ultimately the responsibility of men who have chosen to ignore their guiding voice.

In this universe stars are born and die every day. To assume that different rules apply to humans, or that we are in some way unique from every thing that is around us, shows remarkable lack of understanding of who we are. The belief that man is superior to anything else was born relatively recently by the age of science. This book is here to help you through the awakening process. The very first element of that awakening is to understand that you are part of everything and everything is part of you. This awakening is known to you deep inside and you may have suspected something like this, but have been unable to bring the pieces into your consciousness. Now we shall start to come through to full awakening, because you have chosen to look at yourself reflected in the pages of this book.

It is important to understand that the negative effects of evil and hate accumulate on the shoulders of those who experience this lack of love. Put in more simplistic terms the effect of hate manifests itself as pain in one form or another – either physical or mental. Pain is a simple sign that you are out of balance with your surroundings. At the first sign of pain, physical or mental, you should ask yourself what it is that you should change in order to return to a state of balance. Pain is one of the first signs of being out of balance with yourself and the Divine Plan.

Contrary to what fundamentalists may believe re-examination of religious texts is a vital and essential element of the raised consciousness. Only when re-examined in the light of the new human understanding of how and what life is can these texts be understood as advanced teachings of their age. Little wonder that those who received them found them difficult to understand. Little wonder that analogies were needed that could be understood in the light of events several thousand years ago. These where times when it was acceptable to murder men by crucifixion and where the ownership of slaves was a sign of a sophisticated household.

Today we no longer need to be told what to think or what to do based upon interpretations of ancient texts. Much of the original thinking has been lost by time and repeated mistranslation. Today the human being is no longer a child needing parables or texts cloaked in mystery. It is within your control to understand who you are. You are an advanced spiritual entity capable of understanding your own existence. It is no longer necessary for you to be told by priests how to conduct your life. It is within your power to communicate directly with your God through the power invested in your mind. It is your duty to that higher part of you to discard those who seek to influence you for their own personal gain. Inside of every human is the new consciousness waiting to be awoken. No man can do that – the only force necessary is the one that comes from within you that tells you that this time has come.

You are a vehicle for the creation of love through the will of the Divine Spirit. In order to live life to the full we need to love our fellow men as we would love ourselves, fully aware that we are all connected and part of the same entity. Love in itself being more than just an emotion, but embodied in words as well as deeds. The experience of love is often assumed to be the act of love in the form of sex – especially by those who are emotionally too young to know what love is. This is not helped by the English language, which in many respects may be the greatest of all languages in its ability to communicate world-wide, yet is hopeless in its inadequacy in terms of expressing love as a concept. Whilst the Eskimos are believed to have several hundred words for snow the English have one word for love (as well as snow).

It is only possible to understand the scope of love, and the different types of love, when you step back for a moment to analyse each form taken on its own. There is of course that one phrase which always comes first "*I love you*" – which seems simple enough to understand. It embodies the understanding that most people attribute to the word. It has been sold to us in the media at all levels. In many ways we have been hoodwinked by the power brokers of society to believe that like Hollywood there is only one true love.

That form of love is however just the tip of the iceberg. "*I love my mother*" – is that the same love? - of course not. A mother's love or a love of a mother is a completely different love from that between a man and woman in love. "*I love my children*", "*I love my dog and my cat*", "*I love nature and the sound of the water in the mountains*", "*I love the fresh breeze on an autumn day*", "*I love that book*", Every single form of love is different – just as subtle as the snow to an Eskimo – yet we use the same word every time and do not think twice about it. Love is as great as all encompassing or as little as only just there – we experience it all.

True love is all of these and a hundred thousand more – it is ultimately the whole life experience of love. Remember every time you use the love word you pay homage to the emotion in you that is the Divine Spirit at work. In the later chapter about sex and society we shall address the all important issue of how to deal with love in our lives in a way that will avoid the mistakes of the past. Love in all its forms is the manifestation of the Divine in our lives and nothing should stand in the way of love, if we are to live our lives to its maximum potential.

The Law of Destruction

Civilisation develops upon the study of history and the process of learning through mistakes from the past. We have seen that it is natural for man to make mistakes, yet the past mistakes are all too often ignored by the so called "*modern*" generation. Hence we can see that great civilisations such as those founded in India, Greece and also Rome ultimately were replaced. They were replaced because they did not fulfil the will of the Divine Spirit, which manifested itself through the will of the people. Those civilisations were replaced because they stopped listening to the will of the Divine. To loose contact with the Divine is like sailing upon the sea without a captain. Any ship may do this, but to do so will ultimately end in disaster.

It is therefore important to understand that in order to look forward we must also learn the mistakes of the past by looking back. It would be a foolish man indeed who sought to understand his own life without taking on board the experiences of those great men who had gone before.

This chapter is therefore a reminder of the truth behind the great prophets. Greatness is often thrust upon us by virtue of the fact that Divine Will cannot be avoided. We should look carefully at what these great men of history have said. Any true philosophy should accommodate these writings, since a true philosophy will not be ambiguous. It may require those who look at those teachings to take a step back, in order to re-assess what was actually said. It may take some courage in order to understand what was meant. Nonetheless the teachings of the great prophets must, if true, by their very nature be as valid today as the day they were made.

The *oceanist* is by the nature of the raised consciousness directed to recognise the fundamental truth of reincarnation. The *oceanist* is intelligent enough to examine the written record and come to the reasoned judgement that all the great prophets taught reincarnation as the way of the eternal soul. This judgement comes from inside and is not through the words of priests or gurus versed in the doctrine of several thousand years. The message that these great prophets have bought to us has been distorted and changed from their original true meaning by well intentioned men. This philosophy seeks to reinstate the true meaning of those original words and guides those who seek the truth to their ultimate goal.

It would be possible in this exercise to examine any number of prophets. Prophets are by nature followed by an element of faith. One man's prophet is another man's heretic. This philosophy does not ask for faith, because to do so would place it at the same level as all those who have gone before. This philosophy is based upon the logical examination of evidence and the conclusions that run from the evidence provided. Some might call this proof of the fundamental truth we seek.

Technology and society as a whole has moved on from the days when we simply accepted what our masters told us parrot fashion. None the less many millions of human beings still follow the teachings of Jesus of Nazareth. Many millions follow the works of Mohammed in blind faith and even more the teachings of the Buddhas.

Each faith, being adopted by a hierarchy of infrastructure, has slowly but surely removed humanity from the true path of awareness. This document is designed to return humanity to that path, without contradicting any teachings of the great prophets.

I shall therefore look at the teachings of a number of the great prophets with a view to understanding what they taught us. In order to do this it is necessary to look carefully at what they said and to keep an open mind.

Let us first look at the work of Jesus Christ. A man who through his work and example formed the basis of the Protestant and Catholic religions. A man of obvious immense charisma, who was recorded by the twelve disciples in writing.

If we look carefully at his work through the gospels of Matthew, Mark, Luke and John, we find that he never claimed to be the son of God. Whilst he referred to his "*father*" as an analogy of the Divine Spirit, Jesus was a humble as his origins when it came to any claim of divinity. He introduced the concept of the trinity to peasants working in Palestine. This was explained in the gospels as God the Father, God the Son and God the Holy Ghost. Only later was this expanded upon as an understanding of God being based in heaven, sitting upon a golden throne, as an extension of the Jewish faith.

The Christian teachings that developed from the work of Christ simply require you to evaluate what he is recorded to have actually said. His teachings are not contrary to this philosophy, but endorse it entirely, when the analogies which Jesus sought to use are interpreted correctly.

Jesus employed the reference to "*the Father*" as a reference to the Divine Spirit – since in truth the Divine Spirit creates us all. He referred to "*the Son*" as a means of identifying himself as a human being – a reference which incorporates the concept that all men are sons of the Divine Spirit. He also referred to the "*Holy Ghost*" which is the "*you*" voice we have discussed earlier. This third element being the much misunderstood part of the trinity, which communicates between the "*Father*" and the *Son*"

Here we see Luke in the Gospel explaining Jesus actions and how the Holy Ghost influenced him:

> *Luke 4:1 And Jesus being full of the Holy Ghost returned from Jordan, and was led by the Spirit into the wilderness.*

It is apparent that the Holy Ghost was a spirit in terms of the understanding of that time and as such a voice that communicated with Jesus. This was a concept that was common in Jewish philosophy at that time in history. There is no conflict in this teaching whereby the Trinity is explained in simple terms as; the Divine Spirit that is in me, the Divine Spirit that is outside of me and the Divine Spirit that communicates directly with me. The need for others to stand between you and your maker by relying upon their interpretations of ancient gospels should no longer be necessary. The time has come to understand who you are and when that time comes Christ's teachings can be understood in that light. Jesus was clear to his followers that life was about following the path of virtue. He taught that the benefit of such a path was "*everlasting life*". He demonstrated this through the use of parables and examples that could be understood by the poor of the day, who had little education. Every story needed to be simple and it was this simplicity that allowed the examples of his life to capture the imagination of civilisations.

Today education is a basic right of most peoples. It is therefore important to take on board the core teachings of Jesus in the words of his disciples:

> *John 3:16 For God so loved the world, that he gave his only begotten Son, that whosoever believeth in him should not perish, but have* ***everlasting life****.*
>
> *John 4:14 But whosoever drinketh of the water that I shall give him shall never thirst; but the water that I shall give him shall be in him a well of water springing up into* ***everlasting life****.*
>
> *John 5.24 Verily, verily, I say unto you, He that heareth my word, and believeth on him that sent me, hath* ***everlasting life****, and shall not come into condemnation; but is passed from death unto life.*
>
> *John 6:27 Labour not for the meat which perisheth, but for that meat which endureth unto* ***everlasting life****, which the Son of man shall give unto you: for him hath God the Father sealed.*

John 6:40 And this is the will of him that sent me, that every one which seeth the Son, and believeth on him, may have ***everlasting life****: and I will raise him up at the last day.*

John 6:47 Verily, verily, I say unto you, He that believeth on me hath ***everlasting life.***

John 12:50 And I know that his commandment ***is life everlasting:*** *whatsoever I speak therefore, even as the Father said unto me, so I speak.*

Luke 18:30 Who shall not receive manifold more in this present time, and in the world to come ***life everlasting****.*

Matt 19:29 And every one that hath forsaken houses, or brethren, or sisters, or father, or mother, or wife, or children, or lands, for my name's sake, shall receive an hundredfold, and shall inherit ***everlasting life.***

Jesus referred to the benefits of his teachings as being "*everlasting life*". Only later did the organised church distort these teachings to its own benefit to mean the concept of sending your soul to heaven. A place that could be obtained through their assistance and authority.

Study of the Christian scriptures leads the enlightened soul to the inevitable conclusion that the true teachings of Christ taught the way to *everlasting life* – put another way *reincarnation*. This was not the concept of death or heaven upon high. It was exactly what Christ claimed it to be –

everlasting life as known to the enlightened soul as *reincarnation.*

It would be easy to write several books on this matter by virtue of the multitude of occasions upon which Christ used analogies to try to pass his message to his disciples. The fact that he changed the world through his teachings is a testament to the veracity of his method. Yet we see the development of the ideas given to us by Jesus taken by the Christian church and used to develop a world-wide business.

This same church invented heaven, hell and a multitude of control devices - none of which exist. There is only this life, which as Christ tells us is eternal. Both the concept of heaven and hell are designed to imprison believers in a path of guilt and forgiveness. Each device was designed to extract nothing more than cash from the poor unsuspecting believer. This was a business with world-wide potential, which did nothing more than the multi-national corporations of today in terms of protecting its interests.

The enlightened soul sees through these deceits now and is wise enough to examine the evidence itself. Those who fail to provide the proof required can expect little mercy or understanding. We are not the ignorant masses who once filled the churches. We are now empowered by our own consciousness and the time has come for our awakening. Once truth is found there is nothing to separate you from your maker. If you choose to continue the practice of following ancient practices this is a personal decision, which is every person's free choice. The Christian church has deviated from its fundamental truth and now faces the effect of its own moral bankruptcy. It will not survive the coming changes, as all the great prophets have foretold.

I have studied Jesus teachings in some detail and recommend that you do the same. I was bought up under a Christian teaching. If you are prepared to study the teachings and devote the time to re-reading those great texts you too will come to the conclusion that Christ's teachings do not contradict this philosophy. As part of that due diligence you will also need to study the Gnostic Gospels – those gospels which were banned by Constantine in the early development of the Christian Church. Most Christians are so "*protected*" by their Church that they do not even know that those gospels were written by other disciples, including Mary and James. Most people do not know that James was the brother of Christ or that Christ had a brother and family who actively followed him. These gospels show the true Christ and were banned simply because Jesus taught the equality of women – an anathema to men in the fourth century.

You owe it to yourself to investigate these matters, because it is a serious matter to mislead the spirit in the pursuit of wealth. When this book was written the Christian church had become a bankrupt force. No true philosophy can place one sex above another in their own power structure, or have a moral heart when it illicitly approves the corruption of children through immoral acts by its priests. In separating itself from its own source the Christian church like all other churches has fallen foul of the Law of Destruction and cannot be saved.

The teachings of Christ show us that everlasting life is the true reward of a virtuous life. This philosophy simply presents those same teachings in a more holistic understanding of who we are. There is no physical manifestation of heaven or hell, yet there are many examples of reincarnated souls if you care to look. You will however only truly believe this philosophy when you remember who you are. This remembering process comes with the practice of meditation. Your reward comes in time through the application of cause and effect. The act of devotion in the form of meditation is enough to start the process of remembering, as it is the effect of your action.

Let us now move sideways in many respects and look at a different type of prophet. Christ, like Buddha, was a holy man devoted to bringing enlightenment to the people. Our next prophet is from the same breed of men but dedicated to the furtherance of society. A man who through his own greatness not only knew his birth date but also predicted his death – Michel de Nostredame – known throughout these times as Nostradamus.

Nostradamus, unlike his religious counterparts, had a complete understanding of his own position in life. He was a doctor who treated plague victims, was a confidant of the King and Queen of France, had visions of the future and wrote them down in his book called The Centuries in 1555. His book survived The Inquisition and is now one of the most widely read documents in the world.

It may seem strange to include Nostradamus as a true prophet from which an advanced soul may learn much. It is useful to look at his work, because prophesies can only exist by virtue of Divine intervention. The act of prophesy involves the ability to witness visions in times other than those in which we exist. His life and visions are witness to his greatness. He compiled his work at great personal risk and used the knowledge gained to heal the sick.

Despite publishing at a time when any form of Christian heresy would mean certain death he wrote:

Q2.13 *The body without a soul no longer at the sacrifice.*
At the day of death it is brought to rebirth.
The divine spirit will make the soul rejoice
Seeing the eternity of the word.

A statement confirming that reincarnation is true. He had lost both a wife and child to the plague and paid lip service to his Christian church. He knew from his visions that the words that he wrote would survive the tests of time. This verse is acknowledged by most of those who have studied Nostradamus to confirm the inspired nature of his works. In another verse he writes:

Q3.94 *For five hundred years more they will take notice*
Of him who was the ornament of his age.
Then suddenly a great revelation will be made
Which will make people of that century well pleased.

This confirms his belief that his own works will eventually be recognised after five hundred years, after a sudden revelation.

I became aware of Nostradamus work as a result of a vision which I received in 1994. I was working on my thesis Secrets of the Norman Invasion – a book detailing evidence that the Normans who invaded England in 1066 had landed at a site near Hastings. The evidence which prompted me to conduct this work was received through visions. I had not told anyone at the time that it was these visions that caused me to do the work. Shortly after the visions first started one of these directed me to Nostradamus book, with attention drawn to two separate verses:

Q6.97 *The sky will burn at forty-five degrees,*
Fire approaches the large new city.
Immediately a huge scattered flame leaps up,
When they seek proof of the Normans

Q1.27 *Beneath the oak tree of Guienne struck by lightening*
Not far from there the treasure is hidden.
That which for many centuries had been gathered,
When found, a man will die, his eye pierced by a spring

At the time I did not understand the significance other than both verses appeared to connect to my work at Hastings. One was referring to "*proof of the Normans*" – the nature of the work I was being drawn into by these visions. The other appeared to be a reference to the discovery of treasure. I knew this last verse was also connected by the principals of karma to the events of the Battle of Hastings. In 1066 King Harold was supposed to have been killed with an arrow in the eye. These prophesies were I believe confirmation that my work, orchestrated through visions over a number of years, would one day be confirmed as correct.

That vision prompted me to do exhaustive research into the Nostradamus prophesies, which in turn led to other visions. I concluded that I was being guided by their discovery into understanding the nature of prophesy. I could not effect the outcome, but I must conclude that the prophesy would come true in the course of time. Every time I stopped the work through lack of information or frustration another vision would come to me to kick me into action.

Two years later on 28th March 1996, as a result of matters completely outside of my control, I witnessed a previously unknown comet (Comet Hyakutake) "burning" in the heavens at 45 degrees. This was on the day that I was due to give evidence to what has become known as the Norman Invasion Public Inquiry. The Inquiry in question had been convened because the UK road building Government organisation called the Highways Agency had resolved to build a road through what was to become known as the Norman Invasion Site. I was therefore required to provide evidence of "*proof of the Normans.*"

Although several years after the initial vision the effect of seeing *the sky burning at 45 degrees* had an immense effect upon me. I understood this to mean that time cannot be changed and that men cannot change their destiny. The date for my evidence had been changed nearly half a dozen times by those in charge of the Inquiry. It taught me that prophesy is an instrument of the Divine. At the same time it confirmed the source of my visions. The work I was doing ran contrary to any historical teaching. No-one other than I knew the source of the information which led me to do the work on the Norman

Invasion Site, which I was to publish later on the Internet. I could not have known two years earlier that such an event would occur. I could not have imagined or caused the vision to create itself in my mind. I therefore concluded that Nostradamus visions were from the same source and must therefore also be true.

It is one thing to read a Nostradamus prophesy as someone interested in the general future of mankind. It is something completely different to effectively find your own name written on the page, in code, detailing events of a future that comes true. How men interpret the Nostradamus texts is up to them. Provided the person intended to view the prophesy is the right person, then the effect of the viewing is to put that person on the right path – the path of the Divine will.

Fascinating though Nostradamus prophesies may be it is not in the normal course of events man's destiny to know his own fate on a personal level. To be so involved with one such prophesy filled me with trepidation as to what may lie in store. This was leading to something significant, which at the time I was not aware. I believe I was going through a sort of initiation – a test to establish my ability to deal with the issues.

Prophesy is, I now understand, an expression of the Divine will and is exercised by the Divine as an independent control method. The effect of the combination of the fulfilment of the prophesy, in conjunction with my own vision, was confirmation of the source of my visions as a Divine source – one that could not be avoided, as I had no control over events.

During the course of my giving evidence to the Public Inquiry the other two lines of the prophesy fell into place. The Ariane-5 rocket exploded on take-off in French Guyana showing "*a huge scattered flame leaping up*" on the six o'clock news on June 5th 1996. and "*fire approaching the New City*" in the Los Angeles bush fires.

These matters had no significance to the world at large, but to me the effect was truly deep. No human being had any knowledge of the events of the Norman Invasion in this life. All the history books in the world had got it wrong. I could not prove this but I knew it to be so from my own inner voice. It was an event that had been recorded in history incorrectly and I was the vehicle for the reinstatement of that truth. A truth that on the face of it has little significance in the events of the world. None the less the involvement of these visions confirmed to me beyond all doubt that I was being guided. My guide had a motive and was showing me something that I knew no other human being could know. I was being shown more than *proof of the Normans* – at a personal level I was being shown *proof of the Divine*.

I was unaware at that time that it would open the door to my understanding of the responsibility placed upon me to follow the appointed path. To open the door to my own past through meditation in order that I could understand what I was required to do. It is those visions and my inner voice that guided me to write these words for you. This book is written in a world that is a tinder-box of religious hypocrisy. You do not need me to tell you that. This book is simply the match that is needed to light the flame in your heart that fires your imagination to take you through the barrier of understanding of who *you* really are. The flame once lit cannot be extinguished. It simply burns faster as the knowledge is passed on. When you strike that match for the first time it is your duty as an advanced human being to pass that knowledge on to those you love.

It is not the nature of Divine prophesy to foretell the future of men for pleasure. It is not entertainment and differs from regular dreams by virtue of the content and conscious ability to recall in detail the events. Those who want to know their own future should seek the path of meditation in order that they will better understanding themselves. I am often asked to tell what I see in the future. My answer is always the same – *your future is for you to understand.* All I can do is warn you that the time has come for change. I can warn you that change is coming – changes that are greater than any other changes in any human period of history. These are the changes as foretold by Jesus, the Bible, Mohammed and the great 13th century Indian prophets.

This is not a time to be afraid, because fear is nothing more than a control mechanism of the ego. Fear of the future is a human madness that is as sensible as fear of the past. You cannot fear the past, because it has already happened. You cannot fear the future for the same reason – there is only now. To let fear go of what is only imagined is a most important lesson.

The Divine Spirit has ordained that those who remove themselves from the Divine will be returned to spirit. This is the *Law of Destruction,* which I referred to earlier. It is an immovable law that cannot be avoided. When man no longer is connected to the Divine Spirit man effectively destroys himself. The signs have been set by the prophets throughout the ages and foretold in the alignment of the stars. Those who have eyes to see the multitude of signs that arise now in their lives will see that the time is coming. Those who ignore these warnings will perish of their own choice. Those who come after these events will know the truth of these words and will never doubt the nature or existence of the Divine Spirit again.

Be grateful that you are here to witness these events and have been chosen to take the appointed path. Through your words and deeds in this life a thousand years of peace will follow the coming cataclysm. This book will be your comfort in years to come since it – like the prophesy of Nostradamus - will confirm what you already know – the Divine Spirit is in you and guides you. When that knowledge is in your heart and you *know* it to be true you are ready to take your place in the new society.

The Mystery of Time

It is desirable to attempt to better understand *time* in order that you can then appreciate how prophesy works, the function of sleep and how this integrates with your daily life. Time is created by the Divine Spirit to allow the existence of our separation from it. This can be better explained as a trick of the mind, which allows us to believe that we exist independently from the Divine, in order that we may experience life as a human being.

If you look at how you observe time you will realise that time is purely a function of the conscious mind. When we are unconscious time does not exist for us – yet whilst we remain unconscious it is clear that time appears to exist for everyone else. Every night you go to sleep and wake up the next morning you have undergone a period where time ceased to exist for you. It is not therefore a giant leap of faith to take on board the fact that time is experienced by the conscious mind. When the conscious mind is switched off time ceases to exist – which is our natural state. Meditation is also a period when time can be switched off and the conscious mind may remain active without the experience of time.

If we look closer at sleep from a physiological point of view doctors tell us that it is in fact impossible not to sleep. Science has shown that those who do not sleep die after a relatively short time of only a few weeks. Sleep - whereby you return to the state of timelessness is your natural state of being. People say that sleep "*recharges the batteries*", but in truth it is more than that. Without sleep you do not return to your natural state whereupon you will die and return to spirit permanently. Those who are unfortunate enough to suffer sleep deprivation long enough die, whereupon they return to a permanent spiritual status until reborn.

Sleep is therefore an essential part of the balance of life and allows the global communication processes to occur. Whilst the body may appear to be at rest the mind actively reconnects with its Divine maker. It recharges itself by the renewal of an as yet unknown energy source and gathers the information that it needs for another day. The mind is a powerful instrument, which can create the world around it, in a similar way that those who are hypnotised can appear to change their surroundings and be influenced by others. Sleep is an important function of life, which should not be underestimated. It is a means of staying in balance with yourself. Sleep can be likened to the network connection of the infinite computer system called the Divine Spirit. Once connected you can communicate with the rest of the network at operating system level. That means that although you may not know how the system works, you know that your communications processes are working properly. Sleep allows you to file and retrieve information properly and also prioritise those matters which require dealing with in the life we live.

Later we shall look at the requirements of the advanced human being. A good night's sleep is of great value because the mind can perform its function of communication in an automatic way – the way it was always designed to work. The communications process takes place outside of time and instead of being an empty void in your consciousness allows you the freedom to travel outside of time and space. Many such travels may return to you in the form of dreams and direct communication with other spirits. As your consciousness rises above the *threshold of remembering* you may recall real life experiences from the past and the future. Prophesy is simply the natural ability to recall such events, but in the guise of Divine intervention, which changes the path of the future to ensure such events will happen.

Every human being has the ability to see beyond their own time. Every human being can recall their own past experiences once they have crossed the threshold of remembering. This threshold can be crossed through hypnotic regression, but it is not recommended, unless required to clear past life transgressions. Forced remembering can be psychologically damaging if not allowed to develop at the natural rate. To truly know your past is best left to the Divine hand to guide. These matters have been kept from us for a reason. To seek to move faster than you should can open you to negative influences of your own making. Cause and effect operates at all levels of life – including the wish to know more than you should.

The only safe way to recall past life experiences is through meditation, which will progress at the rate that your mind can deal with. Meditation will open the consciousness to dreams. These dreams will be easy to interpret in the context of your existing life. Each element of the dream being an analogy of a recent event or an explanation of how to resolve an issue which you need to solve. Dreams operate as part of the Divine Spirit's guidance system. If you ask the Divine Spirit to help you solve a problem just before going to bed, you will receive your answer within a dream, if you have trained yourself to remember.

The next stage of development will bring you dreams that have become vision-like in that you are able to recall vividly all those elements of the dream, as if awake. These visions do not die like the old dreams you used to experience. Some will be real life experiences – remembered firstly as parts of dreams or flashes of remembering. You will recognise people in these dreams as being people whom you may know today. Even though their faces will be different you will know from your heart who each person is. This is not unusual, because as we have explained there is a tendency, like the sand on the beach to stick together, for people to travel through their lives in the company of those they have experienced before. It is human nature to choose a life with fellow travellers, rather than travel through life again with complete strangers.

The human soul always seeks the company of others whom it knows, creating karmic and etheric bonds. These bonds help determine future life paths and draw people together who should meet again through the unimaginably complex interaction of life forces. In visions you will recognise those souls, whom you have known before from how you feel about them, rather than the image of their face.

Each life our exterior changes, but the person inside stays the same. This is in the same way that we may age externally, but inside we are timeless, once we have become an adult in each life.

Sleep is therefore the absence of time, which put another way might also be considered as the same as death. Death is in many ways the same process. The only difference is that when alive you are connected by an etheric chord to one particular body, which returns you to that body when the daily revitalisation process has been completed. The fact that you are reunited with the Divine every time you fall asleep is witnessed by the energy replacement process that is almost instantaneous with sleep. No sooner than the process has happened there is an instant physiological difference in the human body – a process that science has failed to explain.

Death is therefore better understood as the natural process of body replacement. It is not a subject to which you should turn in fear. Remember fear is only for those who fear the future. You can only fear the future if you do not understand the true concept of time. There is only time that exists now. There will always only be time that is known to you as "*now*" - in the state of consciousness. You cannot influence the future any more than you can change the past - because the future like the past has already been cast by the Divine Spirit. When you know yourself to exist outside of time, in a conscious state of meditation, then you will know absolutely that death, like sleep, does not exist. Death cannot exert any influence or fear over you any more than going to sleep.

Death is the release from this life into the next. It is therefore a celebration of a life that has moved on. The human heart will feel the grief of loss through the cutting of the etheric chords, if it has formed those bonds with the individual concerned. However death is a function of life – like the snake who sheds its skin in order to grow. We too as advanced human beings understand that death has no hold over us. Not because we believe in a heaven or hell, but because we know that the forces that guide us through life will guide us into the next life as surely as they have through this.

In understanding the nature of time we are inevitably drawn to the conclusion that our existence outside of time constitutes evidence of our Divine nature. If you can exist outside of time then the rules of the universe, which science has taught us to believe as inviolable, are themselves nothing more than illusions. The voice of science cannot explain prophesy and so like many scientific debates seeks to ignore it in the belief that it will go away. It cannot explain time, or sleep, and like many functions of the mind analyses it in the context of what it considers it to be its own physical attributes.

Undoubtedly as we as advanced human beings climb the ladder of awareness we will understand these things as part of our natural function. Many of the things that we have taken for granted since the dawn of science will be lost and a new understanding will replace it. As our consciousness rises we will not need scientific proof, because experience will form proof enough. Science is based upon experience which is repeatable. It does not have to provide an explanation for the experience to be true. In the same way that I cannot prove to you the existence of your Divine nature until you have experienced that for yourself.

The understanding that you hold the key to that knowledge is the first step in reaching the threshold of awareness. The awareness that you can communicate with the Divine Spirit in real time and are an inherent part of the universal energy force is hugely humbling. It takes your understanding of the Divine Spirit outside of the parameters with which you have understood its existence to be in the past. The ground rules of our existence show that the Divine Spirit does not intervene in life in a daily way, because it operates at what I might call operating system level. It shows us that the Divine Spirit is neither just nor merciful, as taught by the great religions. It does not need to be, because the actions of men are guided by their own hands. Either they will listen to their inner voice or they will be separated from it. Under the Law of Destruction those who separate themselves are returned to spirit to start another life.

This is the real world that we live in today. A world where man has separated himself from the Divine Spirit. A world were what time we may have is running out, as we see humanity rushing towards the precipice of his own destruction. The question is can we do anything about it? Under this philosophy the answer is no. The nature of time indicates that the destruction is the will of the Divine. We as humans are experiencing that will and the great prophesies throughout time have indicated that life as we know it will change. It will change through our own actions and serve as a warning to those who come after us.

The events to which I refer should not be the subject of fear, because those things that are to come cannot be changed. We are here at this time in order that we may experience these things which we have created. The reason we, as advanced human beings are here, is to guide humanity through that period of survival. This is in order that we may be truly reunited with the Divine Spirit in a way that cannot be achieve any other. Those who are not prepared in this life will be destroyed through their own actions – like the zebra grazing where the lion feeds. There is no personal guilt - it is simply a life mistake that should be rectified in the next life. In simple terms the mistakes of this generation will be put right in one cataclysmic event outside of human experience. However before that time you will see the signs and know these things to be true.

The events to which I refer will occur in this life and not some distant as yet unlived life. They are the events of the destruction of the world in which we currently live, through the forces of Divine intervention. These forces operate at global level and will be implemented through a series of events known colloquially as the "*earth-shift*".

The earth-shift has been predicted since man first set foot upon the planet and has been known to sages throughout the ages. It was known to the advanced civilisations in Egypt, who have shown on one unexplained hieroglyphic the sun rising in the West. It was known to the Mayan civilisation who witnessed the Fire Ceremony every 52 years, to ensure their continued existence. It was known to Christ who referred to it as the Tribulation. It was known to Mohammed who referred to it as the Last Day. It is referred to in many of Nostradamus verses and is detailed in great detail in the Book of Revelations in the Bible.

Before looking at the earth-shift in detail it is worth looking at the Book of Revelations. This work was created by St. John in a state of meditation in communion with the Divine Spirit. It was written over an extended period and like Nostradamus' book has had the order of events obscured, as well as the use of analogy to explain otherwise unintelligible events. None the less it has remained a part of the Christian Bible, unaltered by translation for nearly two thousand years. This is as a result of a curse upon anyone who should remove it by the hand of the Divine.

It remains a definitive version of the events that lead to the earth-shift where St. John describes the arrival of a "*new heaven and a new earth*". One in which having suffered the events of that time those who inherit the new earth are told:

CH21.V3 *Behold, the tabernacle of God is with men, and he will dwell with them, and they shall be his people, and God himself shall be with them, and be their God.*

A clear statement that the house of the Christian God shall be understood to be "*with*" men. Christian fundamentalists have interpreted this to mean that God will materialise in the form of a man who will come down to earth and live with us – the idea of the Second Coming. This is modern madness based upon the old religious doctrines of a bible written by men in a lower state of understanding of who they are. This very lower state of understanding being the cause of their own separation from the Divine and ultimately the need for their own destruction. The statement that the house of God is with men is confirmation that the new understanding that comes into existence is that the place where the Divine Spirit resides is "*inside*" men, exactly as explained in this philosophy. The text continues:

CH21.V4 *And God shall wipe away all tears from their eyes; and there shall be no more death, neither sorrow, nor crying, neither shall there be any more pain; for the former things are passed away.*

A further Divine statement that men will be freed from death in that their new understanding of life will remove death from their hearts and all the sorrow that accompanies it.

No wonder that the Christian Church ignored the teachings of the final chapter of the Bible. One that foretells of its own destruction and the removal of all religion, as the final act of the Divine, before the new world understanding of that Divine Spirit takes effect. An effect which cannot happen until the things written in that book come to pass.

The Book of Revelations was written by Divine intervention as a chronology of the events of the earth-shift. It is not written in such archaic text as to be impossible for a layman to understand. It simply needs to be seen in the context of life today – rather than some isolated ideological statement. Only when read in its allotted time do the events as written make sense – that time is now - when this book was written. It bears witness to the statement of truth in the Bible and the eventual destruction of all religion. A destruction that is implemented by the earth-shift, but effected through the hearts of men.

By way of example if you examine the start of Chapter 12 in Revelations you see that once the veil of the analogy is lifted the Bible is as current as the most recent news item. It is translated as follows:

CH12 V1 *And there appeared a great wonder in heaven; a woman clothed in the sun, and the moon under her feet, and upon her head a crown of twelve stars*:

An astronomical event marks these events - such as when the planets lined up on 5th May 2002. The woman clothed in the sun is Europe and the moon at her feet is the crescent moon of Islam. She is clothed in the sun because in history this will be known as the time of global warming. She wears the crown of the twelve stars of the European Union, which can be recognised as twelve golden stars against a blue background.

CH12. V2 *And she is with child, cried travailing in birth, and pained to be delivered.*

The woman is about to have a new member of the family. The new member of the family is Turkey who wishes to join the European Union, but is unable to do so because of its own internal religious conflicts and human rights issucs.

CH12. V3 *And there appeared another wonder in the heaven; and behold a great red dragon, having seven heads and ten horns, and seven crowns upon his heads.*

CH12 V3 *And his tail drew the third part of the stars of heaven, and did cast them down to earth: and the dragon stood before the woman which was ready to be delivered, for to devour her child as soon as it was born.*

Here there is another astrological event in the sky where the first line of verse two is described by the first line of verse three. It is a comet which has never been seen before. It is the comet of the millennium which is due shortly – the largest comet ever seen on earth by humans.

At that time there will be an alignment of seven countries with seven leaders and ten commanders who wage war with a view to engulfing Turkey. This is during the period of time which will become known as World War III. This brings about the events of Revelations and the subsequent destruction of the negative forces through the Divine earth-shift.

The earth-shift is a cataclysmic event which removes and restructures life as we have known it. It cannot be avoided because it operates at a global level and it is only within the will of the Divine Spirit that you will survive such an event.

The process involves the planet changing its position in the heavens by turning 180 degrees in its orbit within 24 hours. The forces that bring this to happen will be applied by the Divine Will when the events in Revelations have come true. At that time those who understand the true meaning of life will survive. They will be entrusted to create the new world order where man shall never again forget his connection to the Divine.

The earth-shift is not as some would argue an avoidable event. If it were avoidable the Divine prophesies would not be true and therefore not Divine. Those, who argue that changing our ways by becoming better human beings will change the future, do not understand the true way that the Divine Spirit works through us all. People who take those views still see the Divine as separated from themselves. In consequence they wish to believe that their actions can in some way influence what has been decided as man's path since the beginning of time. A true philosophy cannot change the future, as this has been chosen as our path since man was created.

The Divine is able to influence men through its unique communications processes. All things that men do are done by virtue of the Divine influence. This is the only way to understand why wars happen. They happen because the Divine is on both sides guiding each to their own destiny, as decided by their own karmic forces.

Those who fought upon the German side in the Great War knew that God was on their side, as did the allies. The fact that the Germans lost that war does not change the fact that those soldiers who died received what they always would have received, regardless of which side they fought upon. It is not possible to change the course of history upon the basis that you will change your mind about one thing or another. This is because the decision that you eventually make will always be the one that was made.

Philosophers who argue that you can change the future have misunderstood what the future is. Changing the future involves many decisions which are only ultimately under Divine control. There is in time only one time and that is now – that is why the future cannot be changed.

The fact that we have the ability to ignore our Divine voice in favour of our earthly one is what makes our separation from the Divine an experience worth living. The Divine guides us daily, but such is our limited understanding of ourselves that it will be a long time before we can grasp what we are capable of.

The earth-shift is an event, which we cannot change, but can prepare for. The preparation will mark your own understanding of who you really are, in a way that is an internal commitment to a better future. Those who survive this event will have been chosen by the Divine Spirit to take the new thinking of the raised human consciousness into the world. They will know that they live only by the will of the Divine and will never let themselves be removed from the Divine in the future.

The process of the earth-shift requires the movement of the body of the earth to change its alignment so that North becomes South and South becomes North in the heavens. The earth forces involved are so great that continents will rise and fall. The sea will rise and cover many countries as the oceans move to keep up with the continental movements. Natural forces will be unleashed upon the planet that will make global warming look like a child at play, as the atmosphere moves to keep in balance with the land. Day will become night and the word of God will be heard by those who survive. Winds will arise on the planet surface higher than have ever been seen and only those who hide in the mountains or under the ground will survive the initial period. This will be followed by the period of recovery which will take many lifetimes of dedicated work by those entrusted with the future of the human race.

The earth-shift will occur when the constellation of the Pleiades pass through the meridian of the heavens, when the moon is full. It will be after the comet of the millennium and in the twenty fourth year after the first publication of this book. It will be after the third world war has run its course. It will be after millions have died of man made plagues, the seas are red and dead. It will be after a third of all trees and all the grass has died. There will be earthquakes in parts of the world that have never before experienced such things. There will be global famine. There will be a hail of huge stones and a third of the planet will die as a result of the will of the Divine. The earth will prepare itself for what it has to do and those who understand our destiny will recognise the signs. A heavenly body will fall into the sea causing darkness for a third of the day and a resulting nuclear winter of catastrophic world-wide proportions. At this time a mountain will fall into the sea and the end of our old world will be close at hand.

On the day of destruction the moon will appear red as if bleeding for the hearts of men. The stars will appear to fall from the heavens, as the planet moves through its changes. This is our destiny that has been foretold and is now come of age.

A world leader will arise during this period who will be a tower of strength to those who are believers. This leader will unite the world and lead it into the new heaven and new earth referred to in the Bible. This leader will be an old soul who's appointed time has come. The world will unite around this leader and a new form of government will rule the earth appropriate for that time. This leader will be chosen by the people and will rule in the way that the people require. This same leader was called The Great Genius by Nostradamus and the Whore of Babylon in the Bible. This leader will be chosen and respected by all peoples.

This book is written because it is not possible to change the world in one day, unless it is by Divine will. Those who survive will know that it is their destiny to survive as a result of that Divine will that leads humanity forward. The raised human consciousness will survive the coming onslaught because it cannot survive without Divine assistance. In order to prepare yourself for a future which is so utterly different from the one that you experience now you must understand who you are and how you need to be. This book can help you achieve that, but at the end of the day the guidance comes from within – and that can only come at your own request.

In order to be able to understand what to do in the future it is important to understand what we have done in the past that might be right or wrong. "*Evils*" in the past, as we have explained, are simply mistakes. Mistakes can be rectified and you can learn from mistakes as a valuable learning tool.

Now that we are aware of how precious time may be in this life, we have the opportunity to look at three elements of life that have ruled our existence for ten thousand years. These are sex, society and money, but starting with money because money has formed the cornerstone of the last civilisation.

Money

Money is not as many would have us believe the curse of man but is better understood as *the currency of the Divine*. Money and commerce were invented by the Divine Spirit to allow men to do good. Without money none of the things that men do that are good can be achieved. Doing good is another way of making love greater and therefore in consequence money has the ability to make love greater as well as doing great good.

Unfortunately man has abused his understanding of money. Money is now itself treated as a god by those of even high intellect, because they have lost touch with their maker. They have seen money as a means to make their own lives greater and in so doing are implementing the Law of Destruction upon their own lives and the life of society as a whole.

Money should therefore be seen as a gift from the Divine Spirit with which you should do good. By doing good I do not mean that you have to give your money away in order to do good. Charity has its place, but is not encouraged except in extreme cases where need is paramount. The old saying charity begins at home holds true today as it did thousands of years ago. It is based upon the requirement to use money in a way that benefits those with whom you are in contact in daily life.

Doing good is ensuring that you use any money you may be fortunate enough to acquire in a way that ensures that you, your family and friends make the most of your life. Such opportunities should not abuse others by taking advantage of your money to achieve a greater position in society than you are due. Money should therefore be understood as having a moral as well as legal use, since the use of the money that you use accumulates upon your karmic record. It is not possible to argue at the Divine level that you were not responsible for killing millions of people because you bought shares in tobacco companies just to make money. It is not possible to argue that you carry no guilt with you because you made or sold arms, but did not do the actual killing. The enlightened soul knows that if you make your money from a product that is known to kill, then those deaths fall upon your karma. Do you really want to die of lung cancer because you invested in a cigarette company to make money?

That example may be a little extreme, but it is not possible to one step remove yourself from the actions of others. In the same way the chain of command does not remove the responsibility of those who fight wars to turn a blind eye to the conventions of war, because they did not do the actual killing.

Money is often the direct result of cause and effect. You receive this amount of money because you did that. It is easy to see that money therefore represents part of the daily value equation of life. Money has become a god in its own right because money accumulates in this life rather than the next.

Religions use money as a tool to impose guilt upon those who earn money, as a means to earn money themselves to support their own infrastructures. Charities do the same by showing pictures of less fortunate people, as a means to elicit money to their good causes.

Money was not created for this use, as it is there in order that you may exchange goods and services at a relative value without profit. Money was created out of the principals of a barter economy. A man with ten sheep may wish to replace one of his sheep with a pig in return for four sheep. At the end of the day he has made his life better and that of the man who sold him the pig. The transaction did not originate in the concept of wealth. Profit however has become the god of money and if you earn money you should understand that money should be spent wisely in order that you gain in spiritual growth. Money should not be used simply for material growth and profit at the expense of others.

The bottom line is that money was invented to do good. You should therefore make sure that your money is spent well. Occasional extravagance is worth while, since it lets the soul experience the ebb and flow of the tide of life. It supports the local economy where you spend that money. Money used exclusively for personal pleasure will on the other hand accumulate as a negative effect upon your life. If you feel guilt when you give money to charity it is better not to give, but to use the money in a way that makes you feel good when it is used in that way. By way of example, giving to a charity because you feel guilty may not be appropriate, but paying money to enable someone unemployed to do a job for you is what money was made to do. As a result of employing someone who might otherwise be unemployed you are using your money to maximum benefit to all concerned.

Money therefore induces the moral dilemma of what to do in the event that you are fortunate enough to have more money than you may need. If this is the case it is important that you invest your money in businesses and projects that do not abuse the planet or other people. Those businesses which destroy the environment for profit will not prosper. Those that are built around renewable energy and sustainability are those which do good at a global level.

Giving is an important part of life because it fulfils the most basic rule of Karma – when you give you also get. Giving in any form returns as getting. If you give love you will surely get love. On the other hand if you give out negative energy in the form of hate this too will be returned to you under the rules of karma. Giving away money to worthy causes will have a positive effect provided it is not as a means to seek to avoid guilt.

As a caring human being with higher consciousness it becomes important to give at all levels of life. Giving your time and effort to your family and friends is natural to most people. However it is also good to give to those who are less fortunate than yourself. Many people have forgotten this most basic rule of life.

In order that you may do this money is the most convenient form of giving, because it provides an easy to evaluate value equation outside of a barter economy. None the less giving for the sake of easing your conscience is in itself unworthy of the action. To give because it makes you feel better has no validity in the balance of value equations of life. You may feel better but your money will not make you a better human being.

In order to give to charity or any worthy cause you should use your money for the reason it was given to humanity – in order to provide an exchange of values. This means that if you wish to support a good cause you should be prepared to buy something that supports that cause. This may take the form of goods or services. The element of value is not important, since the conscious decision to receive as well as give empowers those whom you seek to support.

By way of example it is necessary to fund the expansion of the philosophy detailed in this book. This is a project that is not funded by a conventional business and should never become one, because it is the furtherance of natural knowledge. None the less money is needed to carry the words in this book around the world. These books generate revenue to enable the word to spread and in so doing good is done. Those who buy the books may buy them to give to friends and in so doing further good is done.

The principals however are simple. The use of money should always carry an awareness of the moral responsibility it carries with it. It should be remembered that those who have money have received their money through their own as well as Divine will. This carries an obligation to use it well, because that was why it was given to you. This chapter is included to allow you to understand that money is part of the plan of life by the Divine and not a means to make you feel guilty. It should be used wisely if you are fortunate enough to have more than you need for the daily task of life. It should be used wisely regardless.

It would be easy throughout this chapter to transpose the word *money* for *commerce*. The application of the word commerce is the same and carries the same warning to those who abuse their position. The payback for the abuse of money and commerce is accumulated on the shoulders of those who use money in a negative manner. There is no escape from the forthcoming earth-shift and no amount of money can buy your way to safety.

Now is a time for self evaluation and a time to ensure that your life is in balance with your needs. When the earth-shift has taken place money will have no value for a long period of time. The only value at that time will be the value of life and the ability to recover and find food. All the things that you have taken for granted for so long will no longer be important, whilst those things such as the support of your family, friends and neighbours will rise to the top of your priorities. At this time you will look back at the world that has gone and be grateful that it has departed, because you will know the truth in your heart that the Divine Spirit guides you.

When that time comes you will need to consider the future. The new economy will therefore employ the best principals of the use of money and for a certain time be founded upon the solid underlying principals of barter.

Sex and Bonding

In the new society, which awaits us, we have the unique opportunity to start life afresh. To throw away those things which have failed to sustain us and reinstate those values, which are important. The self-destruction of the old will be understood to be an event, which was bought about by the implementation of the Law of Destruction.

Man has a natural path, which we have referred to as the Divine Plan. Those who are part of this plan will be those who are at one with themselves, nature and the Divine Spirit. This should include an element of meditation and a commitment to encourage those less able than yourself to follow a life which is in balance.

One of the reasons man fell by the wayside of his chosen path was to allow himself to be persuaded that he was separate from the Divine. The very powers that he placed in a position of trust, in the form of churches and religious leaders, abused those powers by seeking to enslave men for profit.

This is not the natural state that man should be. The natural state of man is to be in balance with himself, his maker, fellow men and nature. Nature is itself created by the Divine to remind man of his own separateness from the Divine. Nature is the world that we live in and the effect of how we treat it. In that context the earth-shift is simply the effect of man's own greed upon the environment that holds him.

The principal guiding lesson of the mistakes of the past is to realise that man must be at one with nature. The effect of being at one with nature is to be at one with the Divine. In this state you tread the path of righteousness, to use a biblical expression. In the more holistic sense you walk the path of cause and effect, because by being at one with nature you will give to nature and she will in return comfort you.

This is not to say that life will be easy. It is in certainty going to be hard for those who have been given the gift of life. However those who live through this time will also appreciate the value of life they have been given.

The greatest gift is love. Love is the basis upon which the new society will be built. We as advanced human beings will never again need armaments in which to cultivate our greed. Each man will be free to choose his own ability to survive by virtue of those skills available to him. Each woman will truly be equal to her fellow man.

Love is mistaken for sex by the young or immature because the act of sex is associated with love. However the act of sex is not love in itself, but is the Divine Spirit's gift to humanity, whereby love may be consecrated in a communion with love. Anything which limits love is in effect limiting the driving force of the Divine and it is the limits, which men have imposed upon themselves, which have contributed to their own destruction.

By way of example one of the greatest destroyers of the structure of society has been the destruction of family life. The family is the building block of a solid society. Without men to teach their children how to behave at the breakfast table or women in the home to guide our children, there is little hope of remaining at one with yourself and the Divine. To walk that path leads to the destruction that we should expect.

Nonetheless we have seen the rise of the one parent society because men and women have failed to understand the nature of love. Man, in the form of both sexes, was created to live in harmony. He was created to live in a philosophical Garden of Eden, with men and women living together making love greater. The rise of the one parent society is an example of what happens when you move from the chosen path.

Sex is the consecration of love in a holy communion between two souls, separated from the Divine. In practice this means that when two people make love they achieve the closest they can come to unity with the Divine, as an act of thanksgiving. Sex is therefore not something to feel guilty about. Guilt is a hangover from receiving the Victorian values from our parents and previous generations, who saw sex as the work of a non existent Devil within us.

In the past men have made the mistake of seeing marriage as a means to enslave women, by confining their ability to love. Society has been persuaded to adopt this enslavement as a means to provide men with power. This is because the nature of man's social abilities has been developed through the hunter-gatherer principals. Under the new society that time will come to an end, because love is the gift of the Divine to men and women upon an equal basis. Love cannot be used to enslave and still be considered love.

Marriage was created to form the basis of family life. It is a bond which is created through love between a man and a women, which is sanctified through the act of love. This in turn leads to children who are succoured by the woman and protected by the men in a family relationship. This is the greatest form of love, because family love like all love should be based upon a love that does not need to be returned.

Family love had been secure for many centuries, but as human consciousness has risen the need for more love has destroyed the very thing it created. It is therefore necessary to understand the nature of love and need for love. Whilst this may be completely obvious it may not be as apparent to the man or woman who feels trapped in a relationship, where love appears to have failed them. The problem is in understanding the nature of what the particular problem is.

We as human beings have fooled ourselves through the wonders of our own abilities that there is just one form of love. We have started to believe our own publicity and this is a very dangerous thing. Every day in every newspaper and form of the media we are told that there is only one form of love. This love is best described as the *Hollywood Love*. Such a love only comes once and lasts forever, which we discussed earlier.

Anyone who is over the age of thirty will however know that this is a myth, even though they may never contradict the concept in public. Love is, as we have discussed, a multilayered emotional mountain, of which the surface is always changing. Further and more importantly love changes form, as we, as human beings, age in each life. Whilst it may be hopelessly romantic for us to want to believe that love is only one thing, and last for ever, the advanced human being knows that this is not the case. However society presents the absurd position of only one form of love in every form of life. Journalist write about it every day, even though many have had their own lives ruined by such an ideal being sunk upon the rocks of divorce.

The love that comes with the first flush of youth can of course happen at any time in life. For such a love to walk through the door of your life, when you are seventeen is a wonder, no greater or lesser than when it walks through your door at sixty. The problems arise when society fails to understand the nature of love.

Society has to take on board that love is greater than an exclusive club, which you join when you become married. The act of marriage is a commitment to love and care for each other and to built and protect a family. It is based upon your love for the person and a belief that you will honour that commitment for a life with children.

If circumstances arise that change your life path it is absolute madness to throw away your love. These changes may take many forms – sometimes induced by yourself – sometimes by others. True love can accommodate more than one love in its life and as our consciousness rises we should not see love as a means to restrict love in those whom we love.

This is not a return to the free love concept of the nineteen sixties, which failed for obvious reasons. What it means is coming to an understanding of your own emotional and sexual needs, taken in the context of your life path.

Having taken the decision to make a family, through the love that the relationship developed, you have an obligation to serve that family above all others. This should not limit love that you and others might experience. It should not be a cause for suffering for those who move through life with you.

It is complete and utter madness to destroy a marriage because of an act of unfaithfulness. Love is far greater than that and is not a means of control upon your partner. True love is unremitting and does not need to be returned. True love is not bound by the dogma of past failed marriages, but is the decision to approach marriage in a way that is open and allows both partners the freedom they require.

Love should not be used to trap your partner in a relationship, but used to free both yourself and them from the chains of the past mistakes. In society men will need women and women will need men, but each will be free to chose another partner should they wish, once their commitment to the family is completed. However such a choice should not be possible before the children of that marriage are of the age of consent.

Marriage will therefore be the act of commitment to spend your life together in a love that is shared. The decision on whether this should be shared together or individually is the decision of those who take this path. Society as a whole will expect those who make this commitment to marriage to honour it, since it is the children that are produced from these marriages who will inherit our future. Marriages will therefore be more open than they have been in the past. There will be an acceptance that love is a gift that may be shared in the furtherance of the pleasures of life. These pleasures have been granted us by virtue of our own connection to the Divine and a need to make love greater.

The marriage act is not an act of possession. It is a statement of intent. No man or woman should be chained to love that no longer exists. On the other hand it is not acceptable to enter marriage and then leave it upon the basis of a split of the proceeds, because one partner finds a new fleeting love. The huge negative karma of such an act cannot be justified in the name of love.

The nature of men is that they are by virtue of their sex not designed to be monogamous. Women generally find a monogamous relationship more satisfying by virtue of their inner need to care and make a home. These are strong forces which any artificial barrier can effectively destroy in a marriage.

In the future there will be an understanding that life is a learning process serving the Divine Spirit. We enter life alone and inevitably we leave the same way. The experience of love which we have along the way is the only reason we are here. We should not limit this, since the value of your life is ultimately measured in this love, which you give to others. It is the only thing you take with you to the next life. In determining the rules by which you can live this life to the full you must agree the terms of reference that such love can operate with your chosen partner or partners.

Many thousands and possibly millions of human beings have ruined their lives and those of their children through what was an act of love. Society needs to change to understand that the nature of love is not to destroy the family. In a true loving relationship you should expect love to change. It may become deeper, it may become less dependant upon sex as a means of reuniting your spiritual need. In a true caring relationship the need for sex can be accommodated within marriage, provided both partners understand the nature of the love which they are experiencing.

When a child reaches the age of consent it is entitled to leave the family home and set up their own home. At this time the obligations of marriage cease in regards to the children. At this time I see the society in the future becoming more holistic in its understanding of itself and the marriage relationship. Society will live more at a communal level than it has done in the past, recognising the need to look after the elderly, within a family or community unit, as well as the young.

This family unit will operate by virtue of place as well as blood bond. Instead of marriage being an inviolable eternal vow based upon eternal monogamy and ownership by men of women, it will be the right of all citizens to choose their free partner. The *bondship ceremony* will replace marriage and divorce. It confirms the etheric bond that is created between people through love at a spiritual level.

The bondship ceremony confirms a loving relationship between partners who consider themselves equal in all matters. A *partner* will enjoy all the benefits of anyone in the relationship of marriage, but will have the freedom to know that their love is not limited by their partner. In many ways those who enter a partner relationship will enjoy a greater bond than can probably be obtained through marriage, because their love does not need an artificial vow or priests to hold them together. The arrangement which they honour amongst themselves may be as rigid or flexible as their needs require.

The bondship ceremony can be conducted by any person who knows the two people concerned, with at least one witness who knows each of them. Standing face to face the man raises his right hand, fingers together and outstretched as if on a pane of glass between the two, in the appropriate swearing position. The woman then raises her left hand in a similar fashion so that the two palms touch and each finger touches the equivalent finger of their partner.

At this point the person conducting the ceremony will take a blade of grass, or a reed, or piece of string or anything that is or has been made from a living thing, such as a silk scarf, a daisy chain or a flower stem and tie the index finger of the two partners together. Next the witness will do the same so that two bonds hold the couple by their index fingers. Then the ceremony leader will invite those who attend the ceremony to add any additional ties between the couple around their raised arms. They shall then be asked to repeat the following words by the ceremony leader:

I (full name) take you (full name) to be my life partner.
I make this bond as an act of love for you
I will not limit my love for you or limit your love to others.
I will bond with you in this life and for ever
I will renew or revoke this vow at the time of remembering
In the name of the Divine Spirit that is within me and all those present.

When the ceremony has been completed the bond that tied the couple should be kept until such time as it is renewed, added to or replaced. The etheric bond that has been confirmed by this ceremony is not destroyed when love or your life path changes course, as it may do at some stage in the future. It is a ceremony that shows those present that two people have made the commitment to be together in love and that in the event that this commitment leads to children, they are bound by the bond until any children from the relationship reaches the age of consent. Those who do not have children may relinquish their bond by common consent at any time, but recognise that the love that was built by the relationship can never die.

Bonding as a form of ritual does not carry with it the weight of law or the stress of a formal marriage ceremony. It is designed to be freely available and requires no more preparation than the presence of others to witness the event. It formalises the will to be and live with your partner. It does not involve the concept of either religious or state involvement. It is a statement between you and your maker in front of witnesses.

The "*time of remembering*" is any anniversary day of the ceremony, but in the case of those who have children it is the anniversary that follows the last child to reach the age of consent.

After the bonding ceremony is completed at an appropriate time the couple should write their names in their own hand in the Book of Life, accompanied by their witnesses and dated using the words:

(full name in own hand) and (full name in own hand) have upon the (date of ceremony) been bonded in this life according to the rules of the Book of Life and witnessed by
(names of witness in own hand)(signature of witness)
(names of witness in own hand)(signature of witness)
(dated)

Names so entered cannot be removed any more than love can be destroyed and should continue to exist even if their love has changed. The Book of Life remains a witness to that love which never dies, but may change form. An understanding of Love as a bond between humans and its ability to change with age will make society stronger. Women will be free to determine their own destiny with partners they choose in relationships that may be monogamous or otherwise. The true value of a relationship not being any artificial value placed upon it by society, but the value of love between the hearts of those who bond.

In society the love of family and love of your fellow man will be the measure of your worth and valued above all other loves.

Family love unlike that which results from the sexual bonding process comes with maturity and spiritual growth. Family may be by blood, friendship or location, since we are all the family of man. The principal of love your neighbour as yourself being founded in the same principal.

This love that you bring into your life leads to a balance in your life which can be achieved without rules that restrict love. This balance in turn leads to a firm foundation for society to build a new future without the hypocrisies of the past.

Quality

The Divine Spirit has made man in his own likeness. This means that we have been made to exist in a state of balance with ourselves and those things that exist around us. This state is our natural state and one that should by nature be easy for us to obtain. In being at one with ourselves we will achieve a quality of life that leads to certain happiness. Happiness is the goal of all human beings and the experience of being at one with the Divine.

Unfortunately the mistake that most people make is to believe that happiness can be obtained simply by material means. Money has become the god of happiness and in seeking money above everything else man moves further from the Divine every day.

In order to live in balance it is necessary to devote time to yourself. This means that you are prepared to take time to care for your inner self. In so doing your inner self will at the same time take care of that outer self, which has to deal with the day to day worries of life.

Taking care of the inner self is carried out by the daily exercise of meditation. This process opens the communication process between you and your maker in the way we have discussed under the chapter of that name. However a person in balance with themselves and their surroundings also lives without fear.

Fear is born out of not knowing who you are and where you are going. Fear is caused by the mind seeking to imagine what may happen in the future, as a means of forming or influencing that future.

The mind is quite capable of taking the fear in your thoughts and turning them into reality by virtue of the power within it and the way that it inter-acts with the Divine Spirit. Thoughts are therefore in some respect as dangerous as the actions themselves. You must therefore learn as an advanced human being to control your thought processes, as well as your actions because one is directly connected to the other. Thoughts are as dangerous as actions because one can create the other even if you are unaware of it. Those who say that "*thoughts cannot harm you*" do not understand how the world actually works. They live in a world of illusions believing that the mind is isolated from it's maker who controls everything.

In order to experience true happiness you must banish fear from your heart in all your deeds and actions. Once you have come to understand the timeless nature of your soul and the illusion of death, you should have no reason to fear the future any more than you should fear the past.

In order to bring a quality to your life you should also learn that the most negative force in your life is likely to be *need*. Need is what drives men to make mistakes and need should be understood as a false god. Need is created in the mind to satisfy the demands of the personal self – the ego. The act of needing generates the very opposite life energy forces. In needing money you place yourself in position where money is much more difficult to obtain. In needing love you effectively reject those loves which might otherwise materialise in your life.

In order to live in balance the advanced soul does not need anything, because there is an inherent understanding that those things that you need will be provided by the Divine Spirit. The effect of not needing things is for those things to be provided to you. Hence those who have no money cares are the ones who find money is provided. Those who do not need love, because they give love as a matter of course, also receive love more than they could every need. This book comes into your life even though you did not ask for this to happen. Knowledge comes in many forms for those who believe that they are in need. If you choose to reject it this is your choice. Need should be eliminated from your life and in so doing you will be freed of those matters which bring the negative issues into your life.

This is the real world we are talking about here and not some imaginary utopia. The laws of karma act now when it comes to need. A man who acts upon need reaps the rewards of that need and like the Jewish proverb it should be remembered to be careful for what you ask - because you may get it!

The idea that rich men are unhappy has been sold to the general population for centuries. Mainly by the rich themselves, who seek to keep the poor in their place. Wealth is a temporary illusion. Wealth is only relative to your own position in the tree of life. A man living on the beach in India is wealthy with a few cents per day, whilst another may be destitute living in the metropolitan area of a major city with far more money. At a spiritual level the man on the beach may be far happier, simply because he remains in touch with the values of life, in relation to his environment since his need is little.

Quality of Life is therefore the goal of the advanced human being. How can we achieve this in the era post earth-shift? A time when all the elements of life, as we knew it, have been removed?

In seeking quality we must recognise the mistakes of society and seek to avoid replicating them, only to face the same destruction at some later stage. Society has developed from a village society to one based upon city life. This is the biggest mistake that man has ever made. He believed that by making himself bigger and better than his fellow man he was himself invincible and god-like. He has fallen in love with science as an explanation for all things, forgetting that all things of science were created by the Divine.

Cities are the ruination of man in balance with himself, because in a city it is not possible to control the strategic chains of command that guarantee quality of life. Man becomes dependent upon remote organisations who have no interest in any particular area or people. Vested interests divide society and the result is like the fall of Greece or Rome, we have a society that cannot support its own citizens in a crisis.

The world of men has gone mad when it is no longer possible for a baker to make bread, because it is not economic in competition to a chain of supermarkets. It is madness to be forced by regulation to buy milk from a distributor, rather than direct from the farmer or cow because of rules designed to protect monopolies. These examples show that society is writing the rules of its own destruction, when an event such as the earth-shift happens.

In the new world after the earth-shift cities will no longer exist because they will not sustain life under the basic rules of economics. Men will then realise that the only way to live in harmony will be in the "*village community*". This is and has been the natural way of life throughout the world for ten thousand years. The earth-shift will confirm the Divine Will to see this method of living in harmony with the Divine returned to the dominant form of society.

Under the village community the rules of living are well understood. Each village becomes, by virtue of its existence, self-sustaining. Men will work together to provide their own food and operate a local economy that is self-sustaining, based upon barter of goods and services. Local markets and stores will replace the supermarket mentality.

Villages will be managed by the wise men and women from that society, without external influence. A wise person being by their nature one with many life experiences and an old soul.

The principals of free speech will be accepted, but within the framework of the over-riding principal that:

> "*No man may do anything that may harm another.*"

This principal will be known as "*the first principal of free life*". Disputes will be settled by the election of a committee in each village, who will administer justice, based upon the first principal of free life. Those guilty of offences under this principal may be removed from the village. This will be understood as the effect of their own actions.

The law shall recognise, as it always has, that children who have not reached the age of consent need special protection from abuse. Those who violate these laws in pursuit of their own sexual gratification shall be removed from society.

In the new society men will not be judged by their age or looks but by their intellect. It will not be a democratic society operating in the way that men have built the democracies of the twentieth century. That form of society is and has been destined to die from its own internal corruption.

Men will learn to trust their leaders to elect national and international leaders to rule their planet fairly on their behalf. These men and women will be above reproach in their honesty and integrity. The days of men who rule for payment and favours will be over. Those who rule will do so by the will of the people and be paid and looked after by the people to do that job. It will be illegal for men and women so employed to take payment of any kind or favour other than the agreed payments from the public purse. In return such men and women will be revered and loved above all others. They shall want for nothing in their lives, whether old or young. They shall depart their days in respect and honour, with the care and love of a thankful people, who shall ensure that they want for nothing. Those who lead shall be understood to do so with the respect of the Divine Spirit empowered through the will of men.

Should a leader fail his people by accepting favours or gifts in return for personal gain, then that leader shall be cast out of society without a second chance. The position of leader shall have authority over all, but value of nothing. A leader shall seek nothing in return for the use of power, but shall be empowered by the people to use that power for the good of all. A leader who uses his power for personal gain shall have abdicated his power to the Divine that it may never again be used by that leader.

In this way Quality of Life shall be preserved by those who serve men as their leaders. Judgements shall be lawful and just without external influences. Men shall trust their leaders to administer justice in the way that the Divine always intended. Justice shall not be determined solely by precedent, but by the will of the Divine, through the hearts and minds of men, in balance with themselves and their maker.

Beauty

Beauty of the environment should be the guiding principal of those who make the laws and guide men through the coming thousand years of peace. The environment is the mirror in which we can see the reflection of how we value what we as men do, to the world in which we live.

The Divine Spirit gave men a safe place in which to live and prosper – the planet earth. Until recently men respected their position under the Divine and prospered throughout the world. However the recent failing to honour and respect nature and the environment has caused men to suffer the effects of their actions.

This planet, like the stars, is a creation of the Divine and it too has a spiritual existence. It is made from the same basic fabric as we are. It also follows the Divine will, in the same way that you and I cannot avoid our part in the Divine Plan.

The abuse of nature for the greed of men, through exploitation of resources without consideration to the effects of that abuse causes the negative effects which we have seen. Global warming has come about solely as a result of the errors of men more interested in their own commercial gain than they are about the effects of what they do.

This abuse, when taken with the multitudes of environmental abuse heaped upon the planet over the last fifty years, has been man's undoing. Separating yourself from nature and the environment is the same as separating yourself from the Divine Spirit, since the Divine Spirit embodies the spirit of nature.

If you do not believe me then go to the top of a mountain and sit there on your own. If you cannot do that then simply close your eyes and bring into your mind this experience. Look below you at the clouds in their infinite glory, with the blue sky above as the mountains stretch into the distance. Sit and let the peace that is within you come to you. You will then experience the power of the Divine through the majesty of nature.

Now go into the rain forest and stand under the largest tree you have ever seen. Close your eyes and listen to the sounds of the forest. Hear the rain falling through the trees, feel the rain as a mist on your face. Hear the birds and wild animals calling to each other.

This is the place where the Divine exists and man exists with the Divine. Just spend a moment every day to experience these feelings and remember who you are and what it is you can feel at that moment in time.

It was this experience which brought the Landscape television channel, which I was the founder, into existence. This is a television channel that plays beautiful classical and instrumental music to pictures of the beauty of the environment without interruption. It was designed to bring the experience of taking just a moment every day to remind you who you really are. A moment to reconnect your soul with your maker, through the emotions created at the very centre of your self.

Music, unlike the spoken word, has no language, but can be understood by everyone, because it is a vibration that acts upon the human spirit. Music can communicate at a spiritual and healing level, which is not as yet understood. When music is combined with the visual art form it is possible for men to loose their outer ego for a short period of time. This is similar to the act of meditation.

In this state great creative thinking can take place, because you open your heart to the Divine. At the same time the appreciation of the beauty of music and the beauty of the planet remind you of how great the Divine Spirit is. It acts as a daily reminder that no matter how brilliant man may be in all his glory he is nothing compared to his maker.

Respect for nature and the environment must be understood by all men as a personal duty. Each action no matter how large or small accumulates in the karmic record of all men. The earth-shift is the witness to this. The earth-shift has been implemented because men have removed themselves from their maker. They have fallen into the trap of believing that they, through the knowledge of science given to them by their maker, no longer need the Divine Spirit.

In the future all men shall know that the Divine Spirit has cast men down because of their own arrogance. In the future all men will know the Divine Spirit is within them and they are the home for that great intelligence. However they shall also know that the same intelligence resides in all things on this planet and in the heavens. To abuse nature or the environment is therefore to abuse the Divine Spirit and will bring upon those who do so the retribution that they deserve.

The future of the human race is not one of doom and gloom but the one that the Divine Spirit intended when the world was created. One where men live in balance with nature at a personal as well as community level.

Villages will be powered by their own solar lighting, which will use the resources of the sun during the day, to provide power for the lights at night. Power, like food and water, will be provided as a right within each community. The days where basic human needs such as water and electricity were sold for profit will cease.

The wind that the Divine Spirit provides every day to men free of charge will be harnessed to power wind turbines. Sustainable energy sources will be used to ensure that men are comfortable and happy in the new world.

The human body will be recognised as a Divine energy source, through the healing powers of that energy which flows through them. Men shall no longer need drugs. Crystals will be harnessed for their healing powers and the people will grow old gracefully.

The cult of youth and beauty worship will no longer be tolerated. Beauty will be seen in everything and everyone in a way that cannot be understood at the time this book was written.

Life immediately after the earth-shift will be unbelievably hard for a short period of time. Those who will have lived through this period of world history will have survived for a reason. They are the old souls who have chosen to be here at this time to help others and to build the new world without the pain and suffering of the one we leave behind.

There will be a great emotional break for those involved, because they will have to adjust to letting go of those things which they had assumed would always be with them. A great many people will be returned to spirit at this time. This will inevitably include members of one's own family and friends, who's allotted time has come.

It will not be a time of mourning, because there will be no time to mourn. Like those, who are overtaken by events in a plane crash, the trauma of the event will concentrate the mind on those things that have to be done. In any event mourning is the act of saying goodbye. At this time those who leave will have gone by Divine Will and will be reunited with their maker through these terrible days. Those who are spared will have been spared because it is their destiny. It is therefore a time of rejoicing that you have your part to pay in the Divine path to a world that is a far greater place.

Vision

This book is the vision of a world that is a better place. At the time of writing many will say that it represents the impossible dream, because it is believed that men will always carry fear and hate in their hearts. This is because men have separated themselves from the Divine and have not yet achieved the raised level of consciousness necessary to see the world as it really is. When they achieve that level of consciousness they will realise that their understanding of what went before was no more than an illusion of their own making.

Once the illusion has passed men will see the real world that they have inherited. This real world will be a place where men are happy and the ways of the world will have changed. A thousand years of peaceful co-existence will follow, where love is the greatest gift. The lessons will have been learnt from the past and men's hearts will welcome the new heaven and new earth - where the Divine Spirit walks amongst men. A new future where:

- The raised consciousness no longer fears the future, because it knows that it is part of the future, and the future cannot harm it.

- The raised consciousness also recognises the *hands upon the keyboard* of your life, moving your life in a way that could never be orchestrated by men.

- Meditation forms a central tenant in your life, as a way to achieve understanding of who you are and who you have been

- You will achieve the *threshold of remembering* of who you are, if you devote your time to the dedicated act of remembering through meditation.

- Death no longer exist because it is recognised to be the illusion of a faith that was unfounded.

- Evil is not created or blamed upon God, because there are only the mistakes of men, which creates the illusion of evil.

- Need has been removed from your life – because everything that you will need will be provided by the Divine Spirit.

- Love is the greatest force in the Universe and nothing should limit love, within the parameters of normal society.

- You may love your fellow man as yourself, as this is the path that humanity is destined to follow to greater happiness.

- Love has many different faces, each more wonderful that the last. Remember the many faces of love every day, as a tribute to the Divine

- Money and commerce are not worshiped as gods, but serve to be used to do good.

- Those who separate themselves from the Divine separate themselves from God. In so doing they seal their own fate, under the Law of Destruction and the rules of karma.

- Money is the currency of the Divine – treat it with the same respect as you would your maker.

- There is only one just law – that of cause and effect.

- True prophesy is recognised as an act of the Divine, which is sent by the Divine to keep men upon the chosen path.

- There is only *now* that exists. Now is the place of being throughout eternity.

- The tabernacle of God is within men.

- Barter is the new economy and a way to evaluate the principals of value.

- The mind, not the body, is the repository of the Divine.

- The first principal of free life is that no man may do anything that may harm another.

- Quality of life will be preserved by preserving the village habitat.

- The earth-shift as a Divine act is not and never has been avoidable, any more than you can avoid breathing the air of life.

It is as a result of the actions of the Divine, through the implementation of the earth-shift, that humanity will rise from the ashes of destruction, as a phoenix rises from it own ashes, even more glorious than ever could be imagined. Only at that time will the world of men be changed forever and the true understanding of the Divine Spirit come into effect. The event itself is foretold in all the great works of prophecy throughout history.

The *oceanist* philosophy is simply the restatement of those works in the context of the raised consciousness. It is the recognition that happiness is not outside there somewhere waiting for you to find it. Happiness is inside us all, guiding us every day. It has just taken us ten thousand or more years to hear and understand the words that are spoken to us.

The word "*Oceanist*" was chosen because it makes an analogy between the ocean of life interacting with the world in which we live. It also represents a play on words to remind you every day of the concept which ties this philosophy to the fundamental truth of the Divine Spirit. It comes in the word itself *O – C – R – nist* (*oh-see-arn–ist*) – to remind you every day that there is only ***O****ne* ***C****onnected* ***R****eligion*. That is the only element of faith that is contained in this book. The faith that unites all religions to one core belief in one Divine Spirit in us all.

The *Oceanist* philosophy of *One Connected Religion* connects Jew to Arab, Christian to Buddhist, Hindu to Muslim and every combination of faith, religion and peoples throughout the world. It over-rides all religions, because it does not remove your faith. It cannot remove faith, because it does not call for faith. Faith is a statement of wish, whereas the *oceanist* knows, from the heart and the voice that communicates with them, with whom they are connected. This is a life changing experience, which only you can activate or recognise.

Humanity has separated itself from the Divine Spirit seeking to isolate it in churches under the control of men. The resulting catastrophic actions are a result of the Divine intervention through the implementation of the Law of Destruction. A result that can no more be avoided than you can avoid going to sleep tonight.

When men come to terms with their actions and realise their mistakes, then the one true philosophy will be understood. Men will learn to honour the Divine Spirit in all they do. The writings in great texts, including the Bible, will be confirmed and the Tabernacle of God shall be with men.

The last time men separated themselves from the Divine the flood destroyed the infrastructure of life. This was no myth, but a real event, which like the earth-shift was Divine retribution for the folly of those who believed they could separate themselves from God. The rainbow was seen at that time as a sign from the Divine, to remind men of the power of the Divine. A token that has been forgotten by all but a few.

At this time too the Divine Spirit will give men a sign that the Divine Spirit is in them and with them. Those who receive this sign shall know that God in all his power is in them and moves through their love and actions. This sign comes in the form of a kiss. It was given to men before – many years ago, but lost in time and myth. It is a sign that the wonder of love flows between men and women, even in the greatest adversity. Those who carry this kiss carry the Divine on their lips, as an angel carries truth and beauty to the philosophical heaven we call happiness. Men in return shall once again honour their obligation to remember the holy day as reserved for worship, through the consecration of love in honour of the Divine Spirit that is within us all.

Those matters, which we have discussed, cannot change your life unless you choose to listen. Listening itself is just the start. This book is the beginning of your new life, or the end of your old one. It is the beginning and the end of the true understanding of the Divine. Take this book with you in your heart every day, in your thoughts and your deeds.

Remember the words written in the last chapter of the Bible, given to St John as a prophesy from the Divine:

CH22 V11 *He that is unjust, let him be unjust still: and he which is filthy, let him be filthy still: and he that is righteous, let him be righteous still: and he that is holy let him be holy still.*

C22V12 And, behold, I come quickly; and my reward is with me, to give every man according as his work shall be.

These simple statements confirm that in the context of the post earth-shift environment men shall recognise the nature of life as eternal. Each man shall enter the next life in the same condition that he left the last, without addition or removal. Each man only receiving that to which he himself is entitled through his own work in that life. In effect a confirmation of the concept of cause and effect from the most holy of sources.

In order to make the most of each life you should use the love which is in your heart and make it greater without restriction, certain that every gift of love brings you one step closer to true happiness. Listen to your inner voice and reap the rewards of true happiness, through a fulfilled life, walking the path of righteousness.

Open your heart to family love, aware that when the events as portrayed in this book have come to pass, the only protection that you may have is the love of your family, friends and neighbours. The day of the care home, has come to an end. Wisdom comes with age and so it is necessary to respect the old ever remembering that we all age in every life. Invest your time and effort in the care of your family, so that they may care for you when your time comes. This is the wisdom of karma, ignore it at your peril.

Your destiny takes you into a very dark place, where the only light will be found inside your heart. This is not a time for despair, but one for rejoicing that you have received the call, at a time when all humanity will be put to the test. It is the greatest of all privileges to be called upon, out of all the people upon this planet, to serve the Divine at a personal life level.

You carry the light of hope and the power of the Divine within you, which ensures the arrival of the arisen consciousness. That holy of holy beings which will walk the earth again in our lifetime. Not in the form of one man or personified God, but as the arisen consciousness of all men, inside the hearts of men.

This is the true meaning of the Second Coming referred to by Christian fundamentalists. It also explains the concept of the Christian Tribulation in the form of the earth-shift. It encapsulates the principals of the Last Day as understood by Muslims throughout the world. At the same time the 1,000 years of peace which follows fulfils the Hindu prophesies for this time as the coming Golden Age and the Kalki Avatar. It is a time when people will return to righteousness and the world will be at peace. This is implemented through the sword of the lost knowledge, returned to those who accept this challenge.

Every man woman and child who so takes that challenge, either by decision or destiny, does so because the Divine has chosen them from amongst all who exist, to cultivate the seeds of the new world of the raised consciousness. A world where true happiness can exist, where all men and women are equal in the eyes of the Divine. Where love can conquer all and where peace will last as long as men remember who they are. When you awake on that new dawn, when the sun rises in the west, after the great storms of destruction, you will know in an absolute and certain manner, that there is only one Divine Spirit. You will hear the voice of the Divine that has protected you and you will know that your relationship with the Divine can never again be the same as it was before these events.

Whether these events are today, tomorrow or yesterday is of no significance in the concept of time, because as we have seen time does not really exist. You are invited therefore to sign your name in this Book of Life as a witness to your fundamental belief in the power of the Divine Spirit to guide and protect you. Even if at this time you have not heard the voice that is your communicator, you now have the ability to call upon it. Every question you will ask will be answered if you care to listen. Every answer will take you in the right direction if you care to follow the advice.

Make no mistake – the words of this book are true. I, the writer of this book, Nicholas Austin, make no claim of authorship, because every word was given to me from within. My name may appear upon the cover, but this is in order that I may implement the will of the Divine. In spirit I have received these words and in spirit I give them to you, knowing that that those things written here are nothing more than any man should be able to understand.

May the Divine Spirit be with you in your heart and mind for ever. May your soul be at one with nature and humanity for all time.

I HEREBY

SIGN MY NAME

IN THE BOOK OF LIFE

AS WITNESS

TO MY FUNDAMENTAL UNDERSTANDING
OF THE DIVINE SPIRIT THAT GUIDES
AND PROTECTS ME.
MAY THE DIVINE SPIRIT BE WITH ME
IN MY HEART AND MIND FOR EVER.
MAY MY SOUL BE AT ONE
WITH NATURE AND HUMANITY
FOR ALL TIME

SIGNED BY

Tara Austin

THIS SIXTH DAY OF MAY
IN THE YEAR 2003

THE BONDSHIP CEREMONY

I ....take you..........................
to be my life partner.
I make this bond as an act of love for you
I will not limit my love for you or limit your love to others.
I will bond with you in this life and for ever
I will renew or revoke this vow at the time of remembering
In the name of the Divine Spirit that is within me and all those present.

WITNESS

.... *and* ....

have upon this day been bonded in this life according to the rules of the Book of Life

Witness

Witness

THIS DAY IN THE MONTH OF

IN THE YEAR